Madder

anthology 2 / SIMPLE PLEASURES

knit patterns and photography by
Carrie Bostick Hoge

patterns, photography, styling, and book design by carrie bostick hoge

published by madder
isbn 9780692365281

10 9 8 7 6 5 4 3 2
printed in china

table *of* contents

Welcome...

Early in 2014, I released three sweater patterns—Louise, Liv, and Lila. The idea was as simple as the sweaters: Effortless winter knitting for your wardrobe. Each garment was mainly stockinette stitch with garter stitch or ribbed trim. They were wearable si-houettes with no fussy stitches—great knitting to have with you on the go or as you're staying cozy indoors listening to your favorite music or watching an entire televsion series in one weekend on the couch.

Originally, I hoped to release the three sweaters as an ebook called *The L Collection*. It seemed to me that they belonged together, but I hadn't finished knitting Lila in time for the photo shoot so I launched the sweaters separately. When introducing Louise and Liv in a blog post, I referred to them as "simple pleasures." This phrase kept ringing in my ears, begging me to create an entire book with this theme.

So, here we are. Eleven sweaters and six accessories, all with easy knitting and great wearing in mind. The three orginial "ladies" are joined by eight others. And just for fun Lila and Louise were re-written for this book to be knitted from the top down, rather than the bottom up.

I hope you will find the knit patterns in *Anthology 2* to be regulars on your needles—always there for you when you need a basic, staple garment for your closet or when you are seeking beauty in simplicity.

Carrie

the INSPIRATION

the KNITS

lucia

lila top down

lila winter

lainey cowl

leigh

lillian

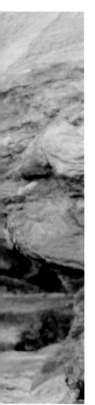

lillian in lark

barn sweater

laurel cowl

liv

louise
top down

madeline

lucinda

charlotte light cardigan & beret

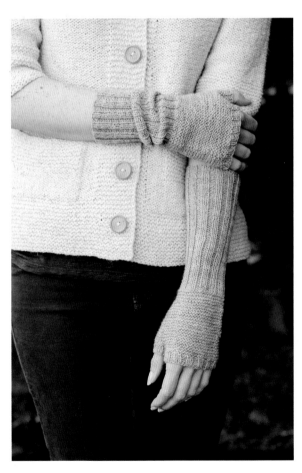

charlotte light accessories

lucia hoodie

Finished Measurements
33 (36½, 40, 43½, 47¼, 50¾, 54¼, 57¾, 61¼)"
Shown in size 36½" with 2½" positive ease

Yarn
Shelter by Brooklyn Tweed
100% Targhee-Columbia wool; 140yd / 50g
• 10 (11, 12, 12, 13, 14, 15, 16, 17) skeins in Snowbound
OR 1350 (1435, 1545, 1645, 1760, 1890, 2015, 2140, 2270) yards worsted weight yarn

Needles
• One 32" circular needle (circ) in size US 7 [4.5 mm]
• One pair in size US 7 [4.5 mm]
• One 40" or longer circ in size US 6 [4 mm]
Or size to obtain gauge

Notions
• Stitch markers (4)
• Stitch holders or waste yarn
• Tapestry needle
• One 1" button

Gauge
18 sts and 28 rows = 4" in St st with larger needle, blocked.

Notes
Hoodie is worked from the bottom up in one piece to underarm with inset pockets. Sleeves are knit flat and joined to the body at the beginning of the yoke. The hoodie has raglan shaping. Circular needle is used to accommodate large number of stitches.

Hoodie
Hem
With larger circ and using the long-tail cast on, CO 130 (146, 162, 178, 194, 210, 226, 242, 258) sts. Do not join.

Begin garter stitch
First row: (RS) Knit.
Next row: (WS) Knit.
Cont in garter st until pc meas approx 4½" from cast on edge, ending after a WS row.
Set aside to make pocket linings.

Begin pocket linings (make 2)
With pair of needles and using the long-tail cast on, CO 22 sts.
First row: (RS) Knit.
Next row: Purl.
Cont in St st until pocket lining meas 4½" from cast on edge, ending after a WS row.

BO 1 st at beg of next 2 rows—20 sts rem. Break yarn leaving a 30" tail to sew lining to body. Set aside. Rep for second lining.

Resume work on body
Next row *place markers for pockets:* (RS) K2, pm, k20, pm, knit to last 22 sts, pm, k20, pm, k2.

Make pocket openings on body
Next row: (WS) *Knit to pocket m, remove m, BO next 20 sts knitwise, remove m; rep from * one time, knit to end.
Next row *attach pocket linings:* (RS) *Knit to pocket opening, with RS facing knit 20 pocket lining sts; rep from * one time, knit to end.

Begin stockinette stitch
Next row *place markers:* (WS) P28 (32, 36, 40, 44, 48, 52, 56, 60), pm, p74 (82, 90, 98, 106, 114, 122, 130, 138), pm, p28 (32, 36, 40, 44, 48, 52, 56, 60) to end.
Next row: (RS) Knit.
Cont in St st until pc meas approx 14½" from cast on edge, ending after a RS row.

Separate fronts and back
Next row: (WS) *Purl to 3 (4, 4, 4, 5, 5, 5, 6, 6) sts before m, BO 6 (8, 8, 8, 10, 10, 10, 12, 12) sts; rep from * one time, purl to end—68 (74, 82, 90, 96, 104, 112, 118, 126) sts rem for back, 25 (28, 32, 36, 39, 43, 47, 50, 54) sts rem for each front.
Set aside.

Sleeves (make 2)
With pair of needles and using the long-tail cast on, CO 43 (45, 47, 49, 53, 57, 59, 61, 63) sts.

Begin garter stitch
First row: (RS) Knit.
Next row: (WS) Knit.
Cont in garter st until cuff meas approx 2½" from cast on edge, ending after a WS row.

Begin stockinette stitch
Next row: (RS) Knit.
Next row: (WS) Purl.
Cont in St st until sleeve meas approx 4½" from cast on edge, ending after a WS row.

Begin sleeve shaping
Next row *inc row:* (RS) K2, m1-R, knit to last 2 sts, m1-L, k2 (2 sts inc'd)—45 (47, 49, 51, 55, 59, 61, 63, 65) sts.
Rep *inc row* every 4th row 0 (0, 0, 0, 0, 0, 0, 0, 3) more times, every 6th row 0 (0, 0, 0, 0, 0, 3, 11, 13) times, every 8th row 0 (0, 0, 0, 3, 5, 9, 3, 0) times, every 10th row 0 (0, 0, 6, 6, 5, 0, 0, 0) times, every 12th row 0 (0, 7, 2, 0, 0, 0, 0, 0) times, every 14th row 0 (6, 0, 0, 0, 0, 0, 0, 0) times, every 16th row 3 (0, 0, 0, 0, 0, 0, 0, 0) times, then every 18th row 2 (0, 0, 0, 0, 0, 0, 0, 0) times—55 (59, 63, 67, 73, 79, 85, 91, 97) sts.
Work even in St st until sleeve meas approx 18¼" from cast on edge, ending after a WS row.

Begin underarm bindoffs
BO 3 (4, 4, 4, 5, 5, 5, 6, 6) sts at beg of next 2 rows—49 (51, 55, 59, 63, 69, 75, 79, 85) sts rem.

Rep for second sleeve.

Yoke
Join sleeves to body.
Next row: (RS) K25 (28, 32, 36, 39, 43, 47, 50, 54), pm, join and knit 49 (51, 55, 59, 63, 69, 75, 79, 85) sleeve sts, pm, k68 (74, 82, 90, 96, 104, 112, 118, 126) back sts, pm, join and knit 49 (51, 55, 59, 63, 69, 75, 79, 85) sleeve sts, pm, knit to end—216 (232, 256, 280, 300, 328, 356, 376, 404) sts.

Work 3 (3, 3, 3, 3, 1, 1, 1, 1) row(s) even.

Begin yoke shaping
Next row *raglan dec row:* (RS) *Knit to 3 sts before m, ssk, k1, sl m, k1, k2tog; rep from * three more times, knit to end (8 sts dec'd)—208 (224, 248, 272, 292, 320, 348, 368, 396) sts.
Rep *raglan dec row* every 4th row 1 (1, 1, 0, 0, 0, 0, 0, 0) time(s), every other row 18 (20, 23, 27, 29, 31, 32, 32, 33) times, then every row 0 (0, 0, 0, 0, 1, 3, 5, 7) more time(s)—56 (56, 56, 56, 60, 64, 68, 72, 76) sts rem.
Yoke meas approx 6¼ (7, 7¾, 8¼, 8¾, 9½, 10, 10½, 11)" from underarm.

Hood

Next row *place marker*: (RS) K28 (28, 28, 28, 30, 32, 34, 36, 38), pm, k28 (28, 28, 28, 30, 32, 34, 36, 38) to end.

Next row: Purl.

Cont even in St st until hood meas 8¾" from beg of hood, ending on a WS row.

Next row *dec row:* (RS) Knit to 3 sts before m, ssk, k1, sl m, k1, k2tog, knit to end (2 sts dec'd)— 54 (54, 54, 54, 58, 62, 66, 70, 74) sts rem.
Rep *dec row* every 6th row two times, then every 4th row four times, then every other row 3 times, then every row 2 times, working WS rows as: purl to 3 sts before m, p2tog, p1, sl m, p1, ssp, purl to end— 32 (32, 32, 32, 36, 40, 44, 48, 52) sts rem.
Work 1 WS row even; pc meas approx 14" from beg of hood.

Close hood

Next row: (RS) Place sts onto 2 needles, dividing evenly and removing marker. Join hood using the three-needle bind off.

Finishing

Weave in ends. Wet-block to measurements. Sew sleeves and seam underarms. Whip stitch pocket sides to body.

Band

With smaller circ, RS facing, and at lower right front edge, pick up and knit 1 st in each garter ridge to end of garter st band, pick up and knit 2 sts for every 3 rows along right front, hood, and along left front to beg of garter st band, then pick up and knit 1 st in each garter ridge to end.

Begin garter stitch

Next row: (WS) Knit.

Cont in garter st until band meas approx 2", ending after WS row.

Begin buttonhole row

Place removable marker on right front, 4½" below beg of hood.

Next row: Knit to m, work a one-row buttonhole (see Techniques pg 95) over next 4 sts, knit to end.
Cont in garter st until band meas 4", ending after a RS row.

Next row: (WS) BO all sts knitwise.

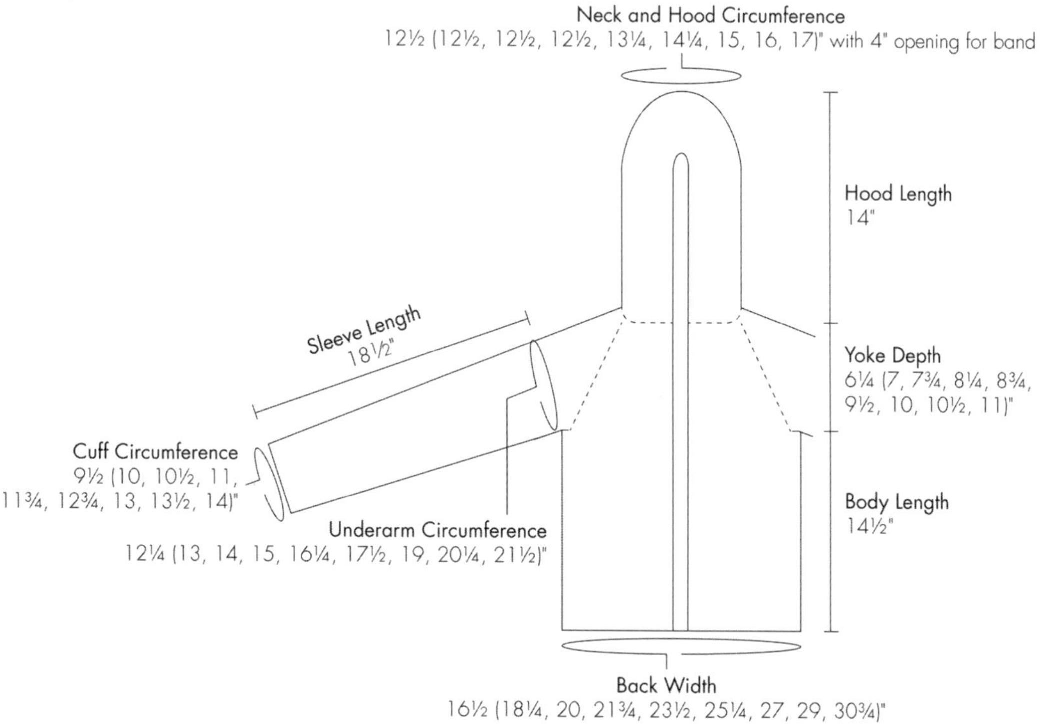

Neck and Hood Circumference
12½ (12½, 12½, 12½, 13¼, 14¼, 15, 16, 17)" with 4" opening for band

Hood Length
14"

Sleeve Length
18½"

Yoke Depth
6¼ (7, 7¾, 8¼, 8¾, 9½, 10, 10½, 11)"

Cuff Circumference
9½ (10, 10½, 11, 11¾, 12¾, 13, 13½, 14)"

Body Length
14½"

Underarm Circumference
12¼ (13, 14, 15, 16¼, 17½, 19, 20¼, 21½)"

Back Width
16½ (18¼, 20, 21¾, 23½, 25¼, 27, 29, 30¾)"

lila top down

Finished Measurements
30¼ (32¾, 35¼, 38, 40½, 43, 45½, 48, 50½, 53)" bust circumference
Pullover shown meas 38" with 3" positive ease

Yarn
Pure Blends Worsted by Swans Island
85% organic merino, 15% alpaca; 250yd / 100g
• 5 (5, 5, 6, 6, 6, 7, 7, 8, 8) skeins in Oatmeal
OR 1090 (1190, 1260, 1340, 1440, 1540, 1650, 1745, 1845, 1945) yds worsted
weight yarn

Needles
• One 32" circular needle (circ) in size US 6 [4 mm] and US 7 [4.5 mm]
• One 16" circ in size US 6 [4 mm]
• One set of double-pointed needles (dpns) in size US 6 [4 mm] and US 7 [4.5 mm]

Or size to obtain gauge

Notions
• Stitch markers (4)
• Stitch holders or waste yarn
• CC waste yarn in similar weight for Sunday short rows
• Tapestry needle

Gauge
19 sts and 28 rnds = 4" in St st with larger needles, blocked.

Notes
Pullover is worked from the top down.

Pullover
Yoke
With larger circ and using the long tail cast on, CO 56 (56, 56, 60, 60, 62, 62, 64, 64, 66) sts. Do not join.

Begin stockinette stitch and place markers
First row *place markers:* (WS) P2 for left front, pm, p11 (11, 9, 9, 9, 9, 9, 9, 9, 9) for sleeve, pm, p30 (30, 34, 38, 38, 40, 40, 42, 42, 44) for back neck, pm, p11 (11, 9, 9, 9, 9, 9, 9, 9, 9) for sleeve, pm, p2 for right front.

Begin raglan shaping
Next row *raglan inc row:* (RS) *Knit to 1 st before m, m1-R, k1, sl m, k1, m1-L; rep from * three more times, knit to end (8 sts inc'd)—64 (64, 64, 68, 68, 70, 70, 72, 73, 74) sts.
Next row: Purl.

Begin raglan and neck shaping
Next row *neck and raglan inc row:* (RS) K2, m1-L, *knit to one st before m, m1-R, k1, sl m, k1, m1-L; rep from * three more times, knit to last 2 sts, m1-R, k2 (10 sts inc'd)—74 (74, 74, 78, 78, 80, 80, 82, 82, 84) sts.

Next row: Purl.
Rep last 2 rows 5 more times—124 (124, 124, 128, 128, 130, 130, 132, 132, 134) sts; 15 sts each front, 25 (25, 23, 23, 23, 23, 23, 23, 23, 23) sts each sleeve and 44 (44, 48, 52, 52, 54, 54, 56, 56, 58) sts for back.

Cast on for neck
Next row: (RS) *Knit to 1 st before m, m1-R, k1, sl m, k1, m1-L; rep from * three more times, knit to end, then using the backward loop cast on, CO 2 sts (10 sts inc'd)—134 (134, 134, 138, 138, 140, 140, 142, 142, 144) sts.
Next row: (WS) Purl to end, CO 2 sts—136 (136, 136, 140, 140, 142, 142, 144, 144, 146) sts; 18 sts each front, 27 (27, 25, 25, 25, 25, 25, 25, 25, 25) sts each sleeve and 46 (46, 50, 54, 54, 56, 56, 58, 58, 60) sts for back.

Next row: (RS) *Knit to 1 st before m, m1-R, k1, sl m, k1, m1-L; rep from * three more times, knit to end, then using the backward loop cast on, CO 10 (10, 14, 18, 18, 20, 20, 22, 22, 24) sts. Do not turn, join to begin working in the rnd, then knit to m at end of left front. This is the new BOR (it might be helpful to change m to a different color) [18 (18, 22, 26, 26, 28, 28, 30, 30, 32) sts inc'd]—154 (154, 158, 166, 166, 170, 170, 174, 174, 178) sts; 48 (48, 52, 56, 56, 58, 58, 60, 60, 62) sts each back and front, 29 (29, 27, 27, 27, 27, 27, 27, 27, 27) sts each sleeve.

Cont raglan shaping
Next rnd: Knit.
Next rnd *raglan inc rnd:* *K1, m1-L, knit to 1 st before next m, m1-R, k1, sl m; rep from * three more times (8 sts inc'd)—162 (162, 166, 174, 174, 178, 178, 182, 182, 186) sts.
Rep the last 2 rnds 4 (9, 10, 8, 13, 15, 17, 19, 20, 20) more times—194 (234, 246, 238, 278, 298, 314, 334, 342, 346) sts; 58 (68, 74, 74, 84, 90, 94, 100, 102, 104) sts each back and front, 39 (49, 49, 45, 55, 59, 63, 67, 69, 69) sts each sleeve.

[Knit 3 rnds even, then rep *raglan inc rnd*] 3 (1, 1, 3, 1, 1, 1, 0, 0, 0) time(s)—218 (242, 254, 262, 286, 306, 322, 334, 342, 346) sts; 64 (70, 76, 80, 86, 92, 96, 100, 102, 104) sts each back and front, 45 (51, 51, 51, 57, 61, 65, 67, 69, 69) sts each sleeve.

Rep *raglan inc rnd* 0 (0, 0, 0, 0, 0, 0, 1, 2, 4) time(s)—218 (242, 254, 262, 286, 306, 322, 342, 358, 378) sts; 64 (70, 76, 80, 86, 92, 96, 102, 106, 112) sts each back and front, 45 (51, 51, 51, 57, 61, 65, 69, 73, 77) sts each sleeve.

Knit 2 rnds even.

Separate body and sleeve stitches, CO for underarm
Next rnd: Transfer 45 (51, 51, 51, 57, 61, 65, 69, 73, 77) sts for sleeve to waste yarn or st holder, removing markers, using the backward loop cast on, CO 4 (4, 4, 5, 5, 5, 6, 6, 7, 7) sts, pm for new BOR, CO 4 (4, 4, 5, 5, 5, 6, 6, 7, 7) more sts, knit to next m, transfer 45 (51, 51, 51, 57, 61, 65, 69, 73, 77) sts for sleeve to waste yarn or stitch holder, removing markers, using the backward loop cast on, CO 4 (4, 4, 5, 5, 5, 6, 6, 7, 7) sts, pm for side, CO 4 (4, 4, 5, 5, 5, 6, 6, 7, 7) more sts, knit to end—144 (156, 168, 180, 192, 204, 216, 228, 240, 252) sts.

Body
Cont in St st in the rnd until body meas 2½" from underarm.

Begin side shaping
Next row *inc rnd:* *K2, m1-R, knit to 2 sts before m, m1-L, k2, sl m; rep from * one time (4 sts inc'd)—148 (160, 172, 184, 196, 208, 220, 232, 244, 256) sts.

[Knit 25 rnds, then rep *inc rnd*] 2 more times—156 (168, 180, 192, 204, 216, 228, 240, 252, 264) sts.

Cont in St st in the rnd until body meas 11½" from underarm.

Begin short-row shaping
Short Row 1: (RS) Knit across back to side m, sl m, k3, turn work, place a strip of contrast color (CC) yarn across working yarn as for a Sunday Short Row.

Short Row 2: (WS) Purl across back to BOR m, sl m, p3, turn work, place a strip of CC yarn across working yarn as for a Sunday Short Row.

Short Row 3: Knit to turning point (where CC yarn was placed), resolve short row for a RS row, then k2, turn work, place a strip of CC yarn across working yarn as for a Sunday Short Row.

Short Row 4: Purl to turning point (where CC yarn was placed), resolve short row for a WS row, then p2, turn work, place a strip of CC yarn across working yarn as for a Sunday Short Row.

Short Row 5: Knit to turning point (where CC yarn was placed), resolve short row for a RS row, then k3, turn work, place a strip of CC yarn across working yarn as for a Sunday Short Row.

Short Row 6: Purl to turning point (where CC yarn was placed), resolve short row for a WS row, then p3, turn work, place a strip of CC yarn across working yarn as for a Sunday Short Row.
Rep last 2 short rows 6 more times.

Short Row 19: Knit to turning point, resolve short row for a RS row, then k3, turn work, place a strip of CC yarn across working yarn as for a Sunday Short Row.

Short Row 20: Purl to turning point, resolve short row for a WS row, then p3, turn work, yo, knit to end.

Next rnd: Knit to first short-row gap, resolve short-row for a RS row, knit to 1 st before next gap, sl this next st knitwise, sl the next st purlwise (this is the yo from the previous row), knit these 2 sts together, knit to end of rnd.

Change to smaller, longer circ.

Begin garter stitch
Next rnd: Purl.
Next rnd: Knit.
Cont even in garter st for 2¼", body meas 16¾", measuring from side seam m to underarm, ending after a purl rnd.

Next rnd: Loosely BO all sts knitwise.

Sleeves
Transfer 45 (51, 51, 51, 57, 61, 65, 69, 73, 77) held sts from 1 sleeve to larger dpns and divide sts as evenly as possible between needles. Attach yarn and pick up and knit 4 (4, 4, 5, 5, 5, 6, 6, 7, 7) sts in first 4 (4, 4, 5, 5, 5, 6, 6, 7, 7) underarm CO sts, pm for BOR, pick up and knit 4 (4, 4, 5, 5, 5, 6, 6, 7, 7) more sts in rem underarm CO sts. Join to begin working in the rnd—53 (59, 59, 61, 67, 71, 77, 81, 87, 91) sts.

Begin stockinette stitch
First rnd: Knit.
Cont in St st in the rnd until sleeve meas 2" from underarm.

Begin sleeve shaping
Next rnd *dec rnd*: K2, k2tog, knit to last 4 sts, ssk, k2 (2 sts dec'd)—51 (57, 57, 59, 65, 69, 75, 79, 85, 89) sts.

[Knit 13 (9, 11, 9, 7, 7, 7, 5, 5, 5) rnds, then rep *dec rnd*] 4 (8, 5, 8, 10, 7, 1, 12, 6, 4) more times—43 (41, 47, 43, 45, 55, 73, 55, 73, 81) sts rem.

[Knit 11 (0, 9, 0, 0, 5, 5, 3, 3, 3) rnds, then rep *dec rnd*] 2 (0, 2, 0, 0, 4, 12, 2, 11, 14) times—39 (41, 43, 43, 45, 47, 49, 51, 51, 53) sts rem.

Cont even in St st in the rnd until sleeve meas 14½" from underarm.

Change to smaller dpns.

Begin garter stitch
Next rnd: Purl.
Next rnd: Knit.
Cont in garter st for 4", sleeve meas 18½" from underarm, ending after a purl rnd.

Next rnd: Loosely BO all sts knitwise.

Work second sleeve the same as the first.

Finishing

Weave in ends. Steam- or wet-block to measurements.

Neck Band

With RS facing, smaller, shorter circ, and beg at center back neck, pick up and knit 15 (15, 17, 19, 19, 20, 20, 21, 21, 22) sts along first half of back neck, 11 (11, 9, 9, 9, 9, 9, 9, 9, 9) sts along sleeve, 32 (32, 36, 40, 40, 42, 42, 44, 44, 46) sts along front, 11 (11, 9, 9, 9, 9, 9, 9, 9, 9) sts along other sleeve, 15 (15, 17, 19, 19, 20, 20, 21, 21, 22) sts along back neck—84 (84, 88, 96, 96, 100, 100, 104, 104, 108) sts.
Pm for BOR and join to work in the rnd.

First rnd: Purl.
Next rnd: Knit.
Cont in garter st until neck band meas ½" from pick up rnd, ending after a purl rnd.

Next rnd: Loosely BO all sts knitwise.

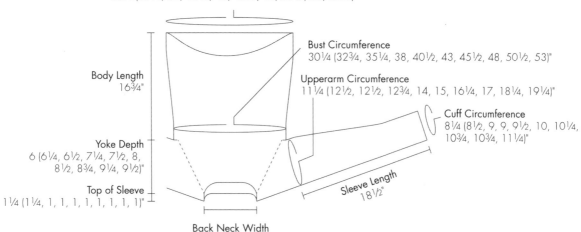

Hem Circumference
32¾ (35¼, 38, 40½, 43, 45½, 48, 50½, 53, 55½)"

Bust Circumference
30¼ (32¾, 35¼, 38, 40½, 43, 45½, 48, 50½, 53)"

Body Length
16¾"

Upperarm Circumference
11¼ (12½, 12½, 12¾, 14, 15, 16¼, 17, 18¼, 19¼)"

Cuff Circumference
8¼ (8½, 9, 9, 9½, 10, 10¼, 10¾, 10¾, 11¼)"

Yoke Depth
6 (6¼, 6½, 7¼, 7½, 8, 8½, 8¾, 9¼, 9½)"

Sleeve Length
18½"

Top of Sleeve
1¼ (1¼, 1, 1, 1, 1, 1, 1, 1, 1)"

Back Neck Width
6¼ (6¼, 7¼, 8, 8, 8½, 8½, 8¾, 8¾, 9¼)"

lila winter

Finished Measurements
31¼ (33½, 35¾, 38, 40½, 42¾, 45, 47¼, 49½, 51¾)" bust circumference
Shown in size 33½" with ½" positive ease

Yarn
Puffin by Quince & Co.
100% American wool; 112yd / 100g
• 6 (6, 7, 7, 7, 8, 8, 9, 9, 10) skeins in Kittywake
OR 570 (620, 670, 710, 750, 800, 850, 900, 960, 1010) chunky weight yarn

Needles
• One 32" circular needle (circ) in sizes US 11 and US 13 [8 and 9 mm]
• One 16" circ in size US 11 [8 mm]
• One set of double-pointed needles (dpns) in sizes US 11 and US 13 [8 and 9 mm]
Or size to obtain gauge

Notions
• Stitch markers (4)
• Stitch holders or waste yarn
• Contrasting color waste yarn in similar weight for Sunday short rows
• Tapestry needle

Gauge
10½ sts and 15 rnds = 4" in St st with larger needles, blocked.

Note
Pullover is worked from the top down.

Pullover
Yoke
With larger circ and using the long tail cast on, CO 31 (32, 33, 34, 33, 34, 33, 34, 33, 34) sts. Do not join.

Begin stockinette stitch and place markers
First row *place markers:* (WS) P2 for front, pm, p5 (5, 5, 5, 4, 4, 4, 4, 4, 4) for sleeve, pm, p17 (18, 19, 20, 21, 22, 21, 22, 21, 22) for back neck, pm, p5 (5, 5, 5, 4, 4, 4, 4, 4, 4) for sleeve, pm, p2 for front.

Begin raglan shaping
Next row *raglan inc row:* (RS) *Knit to 1 st before m, m1-R, k1, sl m, k1, m1-L; rep from * three more times, knit to end (8 sts inc'd)—39 (40, 41, 42, 41, 42, 41, 42, 41, 42) sts; 3 sts each front, 7 (7, 7, 7, 6, 6, 6, 6, 6, 6) sts each sleeve and 19 (20, 21, 22, 23, 24, 23, 24, 23, 24) sts for back.
Next row: Purl.

Begin neck and raglan shaping

Next row *raglan and neck inc row:* (RS) K2, m1-L, *knit to one st before m, m1-R, k1, sl m, k1, m1-L; rep from * three more times, knit to last 2 sts, m1-R, k2 (10 sts inc'd)—49 (50, 51, 52, 51, 52, 51, 52, 51, 52) sts.

Next row: Purl.

Rep the last 2 rows two more times—69 (70, 71, 72, 71, 72, 71, 72, 71, 72) sts; 9 sts each front, 13 (13, 13, 13, 12, 12, 12, 12, 12, 12) sts each sleeve and 25 (26, 27, 28, 29, 30, 29, 30, 29, 30) sts for back.

Cast on for neck

Next row: (RS) *Knit to 1 st before m, m1-R, k1, sl m, k1, m1-L; rep from * three more times, knit to end, then using the backward loop cast on, CO 7 (8, 9, 10, 11, 12, 11, 12, 11, 12) sts. Do not turn, join to begin working in the rnd, then knit to m at end of left front. This is the new BOR (it might be helpful to change stitch marker to a different color) [15 (16, 17, 18, 19, 20, 19, 20, 19, 20) sts inc'd]—78 (86, 88, 90, 90, 92, 90, 92, 90, 92) sts; 27 (28, 29, 30, 31, 32, 31, 32, 31, 32) sts each back and front, 15 (15, 15, 15, 14, 14, 14, 14, 14, 14) sts each sleeve.

Cont raglan shaping

Next rnd: Knit.

Next rnd *raglan inc rnd:* *K1, m1-L, knit to 1 st before next m, m1-R, k1, sl m; rep from * three more times (8 sts inc'd)—84 (94, 96, 98, 98, 100, 98, 100, 98, 100) sts.

Rep the last 2 rnds 0 (1, 2, 1, 2, 3, 4, 5, 6, 7) more time(s)—84 (102, 112, 106, 114, 124, 130, 140, 146, 156) sts; 29 (32, 35, 34, 37, 40, 41, 44, 45, 48) sts for each back and front and 17 (19, 21, 19, 20, 22, 24, 26, 28, 30) sts for each sleeve.

[Knit 3 rnds even, then rep *raglan inc rnd*] 3 (3, 3, 4, 4, 4, 4, 4, 4, 4) times—108 (126, 136, 138, 146, 156, 162, 172, 178, 188) sts: 35 (38, 41, 42, 45, 48, 49, 52, 53, 56) sts for each back and front and 23 (25, 27, 27, 28, 30, 32, 34, 36, 38) sts for each sleeve.

Separate body and sleeve stitches, CO for underarm

Next rnd: Transfer 23 (25, 27, 27, 28, 30, 32, 34, 36, 38) sts for sleeve to waste yarn or st holder, removing markers, using the backward loop cast on, CO 3 (3, 3, 4, 4, 4, 5, 5, 6, 6) sts, pm for new BOR, CO 3 (3, 3, 4, 4, 4, 5, 5, 6, 6) more sts, knit to next m, transfer 23 (25, 27, 27, 28, 30, 32, 34, 36, 38) sts for sleeve to waste yarn or st holder, removing markers, using the backward loop cast on, CO 3 (3, 3, 4, 4, 4, 5, 5, 6, 6) sts, pm for side, CO 3 (3, 3, 4, 4, 4, 5, 5, 6, 6) more sts, knit to end—82 (88, 94, 100, 106, 112, 118, 124, 130, 136) sts; 41 (44, 47, 50, 53, 56, 59, 62, 65, 68) sts rem for each back and front.

Body

Cont to work in St st until body meas 2¾" from underarm.

Begin side shaping

Next row *inc rnd:* *K2, m1-R, knit to 2 sts before m, m1-L, k2, sl m; rep from * one time (4 sts inc'd)—86 (92, 98, 104, 110, 116, 122, 128, 134, 140) sts.

[Knit 11 rnds, then rep *inc rnd*] 2 more times—94 (100, 106, 112, 118, 124, 130, 136, 142, 148) sts.

Cont in St st until body meas 12¾" from underarm.

Begin short-row shaping

Short Row 1: Knit across back to side m, sl m, k4, turn work, place a strip of contrast color (CC) yarn across working yarn as for a Sunday Short Row.

Short Row 2: Purl across back to BOR m, sl m, p4, turn work, place a strip of CC yarn across working yarn as for a Sunday Short Row.

Short Row 3: Knit to turning point (where CC yarn was placed), resolve short-row for a RS row, then k3, turn work, place a strip of CC yarn across working yarn as for a Sunday Short Row.

Short Row 4: Purl to turning point (where CC yarn was placed), resolve short-row for a WS row, then p3, turn work, place a strip of CC yarn across working yarn as for a Sunday Short Row.

Rep last 2 rows two times more.

Short Row 9: Knit to turning point, resolve short-row for a RS row, then k3, turn work, place a strip of CC yarn across working yarn as for a Sunday Short Row.

Short Row 10: Purl to turning point, resolve short-row for a WS row, then p3, turn work, yo, knit to end.

Next rnd: Knit to first short-row gap, resolve short-row for a RS row, knit to 1 st before next gap, sl this next st knitwise, sl the next st purlwise (this is the yo from the previous row), knit these 2 sts together, knit to end of rnd.

Change to smaller, longer circ.

Begin garter stitch
Next rnd: Purl.
Next rnd: Knit.
Cont even in garter st for 2¼", body meas 18", measuring from side seam marker to underarm, ending after a knit rnd.

Next rnd: BO all sts purlwise.

Sleeves
Transfer 23 (25, 27, 27, 28, 30, 32, 34, 36, 38) held sts from 1 sleeve to dpns and divide sts as evenly as possible between needles. Attach yarn and pick up and knit 3 (3, 3, 4, 4, 4, 5, 5, 6, 6) sts in first 3 (3, 3, 4, 4, 4, 5, 5, 6, 6) underarm CO sts, pm for BOR, pick up and knit 3 (3, 3, 4, 4, 4, 5, 5, 6, 6) more sts in rem underarm CO sts. Join to begin working in the rnd—29 (31, 33, 35, 36, 38, 42, 44, 48, 50) sts.

Begin St st
First rnd: Knit.
Cont in St st until sleeve meas 1½" from underarm.

Begin sleeve shaping
Next rnd *dec rnd:* K2, k2tog, knit to last 4 sts, ssk, k2 (2 sts dec'd)—27 (29, 31, 33, 34, 36, 40, 42, 46, 48) sts.

[Knit 13 (9, 9, 7, 7, 5, 5, 3, 3, 3) rnds, then rep *dec rnd*] 2 (2, 2, 3, 3, 2, 6, 2, 5, 8) times—23 (25, 27, 27, 28, 32, 28, 38, 36, 32) sts rem.

[Knit 15 (11, 11, 9, 9, 7, 7, 5, 5, 5) rnds, then rep *dec rnd*] 1 (2, 2, 2, 2, 4, 1, 6, 4, 2) times—21 (21, 23, 23, 24, 24, 26, 26, 28, 28) sts rem.

Cont even in St st until sleeve meas 14½" from underarm.

Change to smaller dpns.

Begin garter stitch
Next rnd: Purl.
Next rnd: Knit.
Cont in garter st for 4", sleeve meas 18½" from underarm, ending after a knit rnd.

Next rnd: BO all sts purlwise.

Work second sleeve the same as the first.

Finishing
Weave in ends. Steam- or wet-block to measurements.

Neck band
With RS facing, smaller, shorter circ, and at center back neck, pick up and knit 8 (9, 9, 10, 10, 11, 10, 11, 10, 11) sts along first half of back neck, 5 (5, 5, 5, 4, 4, 4, 4, 4, 4) sts along sleeve, 16 (17, 18, 19, 20, 21, 20, 21, 20, 21) sts along front, 5 (5, 5, 5, 4, 4, 4, 4, 4, 4) sts along other sleeve, 9 (9, 10, 10, 11, 11, 11, 11, 11, 11) sts along back neck—43 (45, 47, 49, 49, 51, 49, 51, 49, 51) sts.
Pm for BOR and join to work in the rnd.

First rnd: Purl.
Next rnd: Knit.
Next rnd: Loosely BO all sts purlwise.

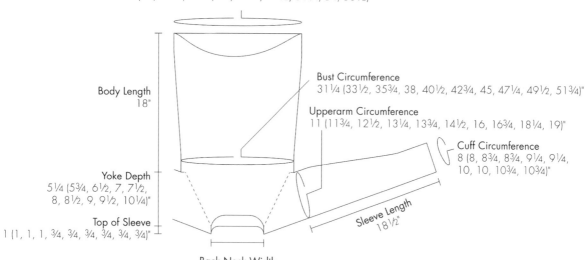

Hem Circumference
35¾ (38, 40½, 42¾, 45, 47¼, 49½, 51¾, 54, 56½)"

Body Length
18"

Bust Circumference
31¼ (33½, 35¾, 38, 40½, 42¾, 45, 47¼, 49½, 51¾)"

Upperarm Circumference
11 (11¾, 12½, 13¼, 13¾, 14½, 16, 16¾, 18¼, 19)"

Cuff Circumference
8 (8, 8¾, 8¾, 9¼, 9¼, 10, 10, 10¾, 10¾)"

Sleeve Length
18½"

Yoke Depth
5¼ (5¾, 6½, 7, 7½, 8, 8½, 9, 9½, 10¼)"

Top of Sleeve
1 (1, 1, 1, ¾, ¾, ¾, ¾, ¾, ¾)"

Back Neck Width
6½ (6¾, 7¼, 7½, 8, 8¼, 8, 8¼, 8, 8¼)"

lainey cowl

Finished Measurements
36" circumference and 11" high
Yarn
Puffin by Quince & Co.
100% American wool; 112yd / 100g
- 3 skeins in Iceland
OR 250 yds chunky weight yarn
Needles
- 32" circular needle (circ) in size US 13 and 11 [9 and 8 mm]
Notions
- Stitch marker
Gauge
11 sts and 20 rnds= 4" in garter stitch rib pattern with larger needles, blocked.

Cowl
With larger circ and using the long-tail cast on, CO 100 sts. Place marker (pm) for BOR and join to work in the rnd, being careful not to twist sts.

Begin garter stitch rib pattern
Rnd 1: *P3, k1; rep from * to end of rnd.
Rnd 2: Knit.
Rep last 2 rnds for garter st rib pattern until cowl measures approx 9" from beg.

Change to smaller circ.

Cont in garter stitch rib pattern until cowl meas 11" from beg, ending after Rnd 1 of pattern.

Next rnd: *K2tog, k2; rep from * to end (25 sts dec'd)—75 sts rem.
Next rnd: *P2, k1; rep from * to end.
Next rnd: BO all sts knitwise.

Finishing
Weave in ends. Steam- or wet-block to measurements.

leigh tee

Finished Measurements
36 (39½, 42¾, 46¼, 49¾, 53¼, 56½, 60, 63½)" bust circumference
Shown in size 42¾" with 7¾" positive ease

Yarn
Cocoon by Rowan
80% merino wool, 20% kid mohair;126yd / 100g
• 4 (5, 5, 5, 6, 6, 7, 7, 8) skeins in Frost
OR 465 (510, 560, 615, 670, 720, 785, 840, 905) yds bulky weight yarn

Needles
• One 32" circular needle (circ) in size US 9 and 10 [5.5 and 6 mm]
• One set of double-pointed needles (dpns) in size US 10 [6 mm]
Or size to obtain gauge

Notions
• Stitch markers (14)
• Waste yarn
• Tapestry needle

Gauge
14 sts and 19 rows = 4" in St st with larger needles, blocked.

Notes
Hem is worked flat for both front and back, then joined to work in the round for the body to underarm. The tee is separated at the underarm then worked flat for both front and back to the shoulders, which are shaped using short rows and joined using the three-needle bind off.

Tee
Back
With smaller circ, CO 63 (69, 75, 81, 87, 93, 99, 105, 111) sts. Do not join.

Begin garter stitch
First row: (WS) Knit.
Next row: (RS) Sl 1 wyif as if to purl, bring yarn to back, knit to end.
Rep last row until pc meas 1" from cast on edge, ending after a WS row.
Transfer to waste yarn and set aside.

Front
Rep as for Back. Do not transfer to waste yarn, keep sts on needle.

Body
Join front and back and begin stockinette stitch in the rnd
Transfer Front sts to larger circ.

Next rnd *place markers:* With larger circ, knit across 63 (69, 75, 81, 87, 93, 99, 105, 111) front sts, pm for side, knit across 63 (69, 75, 81, 87, 93, 99, 105, 111) back sts, pm for BOR, and join to work in the rnd—126 (138, 150, 162, 174, 186, 198, 210, 222).
Cont in St st in the rnd until pc meas 11" from cast on edge.

Separate for front and back
Note: Front and back will be worked separately, back and forth in rows from here to shoulder.
Next row *inc row:* (RS) K1, m1, knit to 1 st before side m, m1, k1, turn (2 sts inc'd)—65 (71, 77, 83, 89, 95, 101, 107, 113) sts for front. Remove markers and place 63 (69, 75, 81, 87, 93, 99, 105, 111) back sts onto waste yarn.
Turn work to begin working back and forth in rows.

Front
Begin stockinette stitch, flat
Next row: (WS) Purl.
Next row: (RS) Knit.
Cont in St st until pc meas 5 (5¼, 5½, 6, 6¼, 6½, 7, 7¼, 7¾)" from underarm, ending after a RS row.

Begin garter stitch, flat
Next row: (WS) Knit.
Cont in gartert st until pc meas 6 (6¼, 6½, 7, 7¼, 7½, 8, 8¼, 8¾)" from underarm, ending after a RS row.

Next row *place markers:* (WS) K2 (2, 3, 3, 3, 4, 4, 4, 5), pm, k2 (2, 3, 3, 3, 4, 4, 5, 5), pm, k2 (2, 3, 3, 4, 4, 4, 5, 5), pm, k2 (3, 3, 3, 4, 4, 5, 5, 5), pm, k2 (3, 3, 4, 4, 4, 5, 5, 5), pm, k3 (3, 3, 4, 4, 4, 5, 5, 6), pm, k3 (3, 3, 4, 4, 5, 5, 5, 6), pm, k33 (35, 35, 35, 37, 37, 37, 39, 39), pm, k3 (3, 3, 4, 4, 5, 5, 5, 6), pm, k3 (3, 3, 4, 4, 4, 5, 5, 6), pm, k2 (3, 3, 4, 4, 4, 5, 5, 5), pm, k2 (3, 3, 3, 4, 4, 5, 5, 5), pm, k2 (2, 3, 3, 4, 4, 4, 5, 5), pm, k2 (2, 3, 3, 3, 4, 4, 5, 5), pm, knit rem 2 (2, 3, 3, 3, 4, 4, 4, 5) sts.

Begin short row shoulder shaping
Short Row 1: (RS) Knit to last marker, remove m, wrap and turn.
Short Row 2: (WS) Knit to last marker, remove m, wrap and turn.
Rep Short Rows 1 and 2 six more times.

Next row: (RS) Knit and place markers between center 27 (29, 29, 29, 31, 31, 31, 33, 33) sts.
Next row: (WS) Knit, binding off neck sts between markers, knit to end.

Back
Slip sts to working needle ready to work a WS row. Rep as for front.

Finishing
Block pcs to measurements. Use the three-needle bind off to join shoulder sts together.

Begin neckband
With smaller circ and RS facing, at center back neck, pick up and knit st for st along neck edge for 54 (58, 58, 58, 62, 62, 62, 66, 66) sts. Join to work in the rnd, pm for BOR.

Next rnd: Loosely BO all sts knitwise.

Begin cuff edging
With dpns, at lower edge of sleeve with RS facing, pick up and knit 2 sts for every 3 rows all around.
Next rnd: Loosely BO all sts knitwise.

Rep on second sleeve.

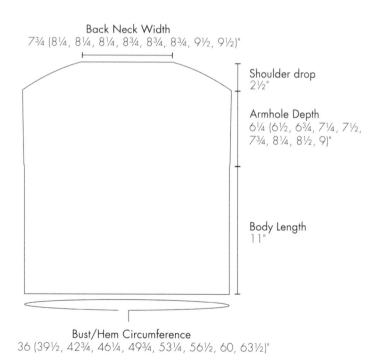

Back Neck Width
7¾ (8¼, 8¼, 8¼, 8¾, 8¾, 8¾, 9½, 9½)"

Shoulder drop
2½"

Armhole Depth
6¼ (6½, 6¾, 7¼, 7½,
7¾, 8¼, 8½, 9)"

Body Length
11"

Bust/Hem Circumference
36 (39½, 42¾, 46¼, 49¾, 53¼, 56½, 60, 63½)"

lillian

Finished Measurements
32¾ (36¼, 39½, 43, 47¼, 50½, 53, 56½, 59¾)" at bust
Shown in size 36¼" with 3¼" positive ease

Yarn
Primo Worsted by The Plucky Knitter
75% merino, 20% cashmere, 5% nylon; 200yd / 100g
• 6 (6, 7, 7, 8, 8, 9, 9, 10) skeins in Fisherman's Wharf
OR 1080 (1140, 1255, 1350, 1430, 1540, 1635, 1760, 1865) yds worsted weight yarn
• Also shown in Lark by Quince & Co. in Chanterelle, read more in Notes about this version.

Needles
• One 16" and 32" circular needle (circ) in size US 7 [4.5 mm]
• One pair in size US 7 [4.5 mm]
Or size to obtain gauge

Notions
• Stitch markers
• Stitch holder or waste yarn
• Tapestry needle

Gauge
19 sts and 29 rows = 4" in St st, blocked.

Notes
Cardi body and sleeves are worked back and forth in rows from the top down. Circular needle is used to accommodate large number of stitches. Band is picked up and worked after body is complete.

Also shown on pages 26–27 is a version of Lillian in Lark yarn worked at the same gauge. The cardi is worked in Rev St st; raglan inc rows are made as follows: *Purl to 2 sts before m, p1-f/b, p1, sl m, p1, p1-f/b; rep from * three more times, purl to end. For side shaping increases, substitute m1-R and m1-L with m1-P. For sleeve decreases, substitute ssk with ssp, and k2tog with p2tog.

Cardi
Yoke
With shorter circ, CO 54 sts. Do not join.

Begin stockinette stitch
First row *place markers:* (WS) K2 for front, pm, k10 (8, 8, 8, 6, 6, 6, 6, 6) for sleeve, pm, k30 (34, 34, 34, 38, 38, 38, 38, 38) for back, pm, k10 (8, 8, 8, 6, 6, 6, 6, 6) for sleeve, pm, k2 for front.

Begin raglan shaping
Note: Change to longer circ when necessary.
First row *inc row:* (RS) *Knit to 1 st before m, k1-r/b, sl m, k1, k1-r/b; rep from * three more times (8 sts inc'd)—62 sts.

Next row: Purl.

Rep *inc row* every other row 17 (20, 23, 25, 26, 24, 27, 29, 28) more times, every 4th row 2 (1, 1, 0, 0, 0, 0, 0, 0) time(s), then every row 0 (0, 0, 1, 1, 6, 5, 5, 8) time(s); working WS rows as *purl to 1 st before m, p1-f/b, sl m, p1, p1-f/b; rep from * three more times, purl to end—214 (230, 254, 270, 278, 302, 318, 334, 350) sts.

For Sizes 32¾ and 36¼"

Skip to All Sizes below.

For Sizes – (-, 39½, 43, 47¼, 50½, 53, 56½, 59¾)"

Next row *body only inc row:* *Work to 1 st before m, k1-r/b, sl m, work to next m, sl m, k1, k1-r/b; rep from * one more time (4 sts inc'd)— - (-, 258, 274, 282, 306, 322, 338, 354) sts.

Rep *body only inc row* every row - (-, 0, 2, 3, 4, 4, 6, 8) more times— - (-, 258, 282, 294, 322, 338, 362, 386) sts.

All Sizes:

22 (24, 28, 32, 34, 38, 40, 44, 48) sts for each front, 70 (78, 86, 94, 102, 110, 114, 122, 130) sts for back, 50 (52, 58, 62, 62, 68, 72, 76, 80) sts for each sleeve.

Purl 1 WS row; yoke meas approx 6¼ (6½, 7½, 7¾, 8¼, 8½, 9¼, 10, 10½)" from cast on edge.

Begin underarm cast-on

Next row: (RS) Knit front sts to m, remove m, transfer next 50 (52, 58, 62, 62, 68, 72, 76, 80) sleeve sts to stitch holder or waste yarn, remove m, using backward loop cast on, CO 4 (4, 4, 4, 5, 5, 6, 6, 6) underarm sts, pm for side, CO 4 (4, 4, 4, 5, 5, 6, 6, 6) more sts, knit back sts to m, remove m, transfer next 50 (52, 58, 62, 62, 68, 72, 76, 80) sleeve sts to stitch holder or waste yarn, remove m, using the backward loop cast on, CO 4 (4, 4, 4, 5, 5, 6, 6, 6) underarm sts, pm for side, CO 4 (4, 4, 4, 5, 5, 6, 6, 6) more sts, knit front sts to end—130 (142, 158, 174, 190, 206, 218, 234, 250) sts on needle.

Body

Cont in St st until body meas approx 2" from underarm cast on, ending after a WS row.

Begin side shaping

Next row *inc row:* (RS) *Knit to 2 sts before m, m1-R, k2, sl m, k2, m1-L; rep from * one time, knit to end (4 sts inc'd)—134 (146, 162, 178, 194, 210, 222, 238, 254) sts.

Rep *inc row* every 20th row three more times—146 (158, 174, 190, 206, 222, 234, 250, 266) sts.

Cont in St st until body meas approx 15" from underarm cast on, ending after a WS row.

Begin garter stitch

Next row: (RS) Knit.

Next row: (WS) Knit.

Cont in garter st until body meas 17" from underarm cast on, ending after a RS row.

Next row: (WS) Loosely BO sts knitwise.

Sleeves

Note: Change to straight needles when comfortable, if desired.

With shorter circ, transfer 50 (52, 58, 62, 62, 68, 72, 76, 80) sleeve sts from stitch holder or waste yarn to needle, do not join.

Begin underarm shaping

Next row: (RS) Using the backward loop cast on, CO 4 (4, 4, 4, 5, 5, 6, 6, 6) sts, knit to end.

Next row: (WS) Using the backward loop cast on, CO 4 (4, 4, 4, 5, 5, 6, 6, 6) sts, purl to end—58 (60, 66, 70, 72, 78, 84, 88, 92) sts.

Cont in St st until sleeve meas approx 1½ (1½, 1½, 1½, 1½, 1, 1, 1, 1)", ending after a WS row.

Begin sleeve shaping

Next row *dec row:* (RS) K2, ssk, knit to last 4 sts, k2tog, k2 (2 sts dec'd)—56 (58, 64, 70, 76, 82, 86, 90) sts.

Rep *dec row* every 12th row 5 (0, 0, 0, 0, 0, 0, 0, 0), every 10th row 2 (8, 0, 0, 0, 0, 0, 0, 0) more times, every 8th row 0 (0, 7, 7, 4, 3, 0, 0, 0) times, every 6th row 0 (0, 4, 4, 8, 10, 10, 10, 6) times, then every 4th row 0 (0, 0, 0, 0, 0, 6, 6, 12) times—42 (42, 42, 46, 46, 50, 50, 54, 54) sts rem.

Cont even in St st until sleeve meas approx 13½" from underarm, ending after a WS row.

Begin 2x2 cuff
Next row: (RS) K1, *k2, p2; rep from * to last st, k1.
Next row: P1, *k2, p2; rep from * to last st, p1.
Cont 2x2 rib as est until cuff meas 4¼"; sleeve meas approx 17¾" from underarm, ending after a WS row.

Next row: (RS) Loosely BO all sts in pattern.

Begin pockets (make 2)
With pair of needles, CO 24 sts.

Begin garter stitch
First row: (RS) Knit.
Cont in garter st until pocket meas approx 4¼" from cast on edge, ending after a WS row.

Begin 2x2 rib
Next row: (RS) K1, *k2, p2; rep from * to last 3 sts, k3.
Next row: P1, * p2, k2: rep from * to last 3 sts, p3.
Cont in 2x2 rib until pocket meas 4¾" from cast on edge, ending after a WS row.

Next row: (RS) BO all sts in pattern.

Finishing
Weave in ends. Wet-block all pcs to measurements. Sew one pocket to each side of body. Seam sleeves and underarms.

Band
With longer circ, RS facing, and at the lower edge of right front, pick up and knit 2 sts for every 3 rows across right front, stitch for stitch around neck, and 2 sts for every 3 rows down the left front, making sure you end up with a multiple of 4 sts.

Pick up and knit 111 (113, 117, 119, 121, 123, 125, 127, 131) sts for each front, 54 sts along neck— 276 (280, 288, 292, 296, 300, 304, 308, 316) sts

Begin 2x2 rib
First row: (WS) P1, *p2, k2; rep from * to last 3 sts, p3.
Next row: (RS) K1, *k2, p2; rep from * to last 3 sts, k3.
Cont in rib as est until band meas 4" from pick up edge.

Next row: (WS) Loosely BO all sts in pattern.

Weave in loose ends. Block again.

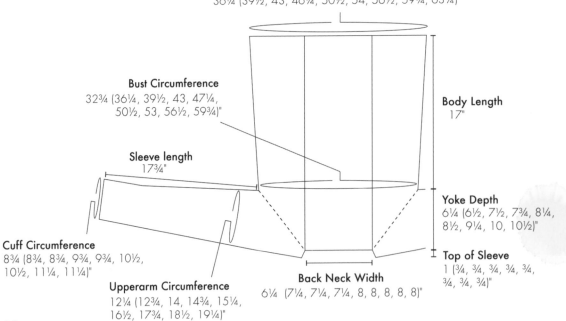

Hem Circumference
36¼ (39½, 43, 46¼, 50½, 54, 56½, 59¾, 63¼)"

Bust Circumference
32¾ (36¼, 39½, 43, 47¼, 50½, 53, 56½, 59¾)"

Body Length
17"

Sleeve length
17¾"

Yoke Depth
6¼ (6½, 7½, 7¾, 8¼, 8½, 9¼, 10, 10½)"

Cuff Circumference
8¾ (8¾, 8¾, 9¾, 9¾, 10½, 10½, 11¼, 11¼)"

Top of Sleeve
1 (¾, ¾, ¾, ¾, ¾, ¾, ¾, ¾)"

Upperarm Circumference
12¼ (12¾, 14, 14¾, 15¼, 16½, 17¾, 18½, 19¼)"

Back Neck Width
6¼ (7¼, 7¼, 7¼, 8, 8, 8, 8, 8)"

barn sweater

Finished Measurements
31 (34¾, 38¼, 42¾, 46¼, 49¾, 53¼)"
buttoned at bust, with 2¾" overlapping button band
Shown in size 34¾" above with 1¾" positive ease
and on pages 28–29 with ¾" positive ease

Yarn
Owl by Quince & Co.
50% American wool, 50% Alpaca; 120yd / 50g
Shown in Buru
For ¾ length sleeves: 9 (10, 11, 12, 13, 14, 15)
skeins
OR 1080 (1200, 1320, 1440, 1560, 1680,
1800) yds worsted weight yarn
For full length sleeves: 10 (11, 12, 13, 14, 15,
17) skeins
OR 1200 (1320, 1440, 1560, 1680, 1800,
2040) yds worsted weight yarn

Needles
• One 32" circular needle (circ) in size US 6
  and 7 [4 and 4.5 mm]
• One pair in size US 6 and 7 [4 and 4.5 mm]
Or size to obtain gauge

Notions
• Stitch markers (6)
• Stitch holders or waste yarn
• Tapestry needle
• Seven 1" buttons

Gauge
18 sts and 26 rows = 4" in Rev St st with larger
needle, blocked.

Reverse stockinette stitch
Purl on RS, knit on WS.

Notes
Cardigan is worked from the top down. Circular
needle is used to accommodate large number
of stitches.
Work slipped stitches with yarn in back as if to knit.
To easily tell RS from WS, it may be beneficial to
place a marker or a piece of waste yarn into RS
when working in garter st.
It is suggested to use different colored markers for
the bands than for the raglan, sides and pockets, to
easily tell them apart.
Two sleeve length options are available. Be sure to
purchase the correct amount of yarn for the sleeve
option you choose.

Cardigan
Collar
With larger circ and using the long-tail cast on, CO
76 (80, 88, 88, 96, 102, 108) sts. Do not join.

Begin garter stitch collar
First row: (RS) Sl 1 wyib as if to knit, knit to end.
Rep last row until collar meas approx 2" from cast on edge.

Change to smaller circ.

Cont in garter st and slipping first st as est until pc meas approx 5" from cast on edge, ending after a WS row.

Sizes 31 (34¾, 38¼, 42¾, 46¼, -, -)" only:
Knit 1 RS row.

Sizes - (-, -, -, -, 49¾, 53¼)" only:
Next row *inc row:* (RS) K- (-, -, -, -, 31, 34), *k1-f/b, k- (-, -, -, -, 38, 12); rep from * - (-, -, -, -, 0, 2) more times, k1-f/b, knit to end— - (-, -, -, -, 104, 112) sts.

All sizes:
Change to larger circ.

Yoke
Begin garter stitch bands and Rev St st yoke
First row *place markers:* (WS) Sl1, k11 for band, pm for band, k6 (8, 10, 11, 13, 15, 17) for right front, pm for raglan, k8 (6, 6, 4, 4, 4, 4) for sleeve, pm for raglan, k24 (28, 32, 34, 38, 42, 46) for back, pm for raglan, k8 (6, 6, 4, 4, 4, 4) for sleeve, pm for raglan, k6 (8, 10, 11, 13, 15, 17) for left front, pm for band, k12 for band.

Shape raglan
Note: Read the following instructions carefully before beginning: buttonholes are worked at the same time as the raglan shaping. Raglan shaping is completed before all the buttonholes are worked. Cont working buttonholes while working the body.

Next row *inc row:* (RS) *Work to 2 sts before raglan marker, p1-f/b, p1, sl m, p1, p1-f/b; rep from * 3 more times, work to end as est (8 sts inc'd)—84 (88, 96, 96, 104, 112, 120) sts.
Work 1 WS row even as est, keeping band sts in garter st and all other sts in Rev St st.
Rep the last 2 rows 18 (19, 21, 24, 26, 27, 29) more times; **and at the same time,** when yoke meas approx 1" (approx 6" from cast on edge), ending after a WS row, begin buttonholes.

Buttonhole row 1: (RS) Work as est to last 8 sts k2tog, [yo] two times, k2tog, work to end as est.
Buttonhole row 2: (WS) Work as est to buttonhole, knit into yo, knit into back of extra wrap, knit to end.

Work 22 (22, 22, 24, 24, 24, 26) rows as est.
Rep *buttonhole rows 1 and 2.*
Rep last 24 (24, 24, 26, 26, 26, 28) rows 5 more times (7 buttonholes total).

When all raglan shaping is complete there are 228 (240, 264, 288, 312, 328, 352) total sts; 62 (68, 76, 84, 92, 98, 106) back sts, 46 (46, 50, 54, 58, 60, 64) sleeve sts, and 37 (40, 44, 48, 52, 55, 59) front sts.

Cast on for underarm
Next row: (RS) Work to first raglan m, remove m, slip next 46 (46, 50, 54, 58, 60, 64) sleeve sts to st holder or waste yarn, remove m, using the backward loop cast on, CO 4 (5, 5, 6, 6, 7, 7) sts, pm for side, CO 4 (5, 5, 6, 6, 7, 7) more sts, work across back sts to next raglan m, remove m, slip next 46 (46, 50, 54, 58, 60, 64) sleeve sts to st holder or waste yarn, remove m, using the backward loop cast on, CO 4 (5, 5, 6, 6, 7, 7) sts, pm for side, CO 4 (5, 5, 6, 6, 7, 7) more sts, work to end as est—152 (168, 184, 204, 220, 236, 252) body sts rem on needle.

Body
Cont as est working body in Rev St st and bands in garter st until body meas approx 2" from underarm, ending after a WS row.

Begin side shaping
Next row *inc row:* (RS) *Work as est to 3 sts before side m, p1-f/b, p2, sl m, p2, p1-f/b; rep from * one more time, work to end as est (4 sts inc'd)—156 (172, 188, 208, 224, 240, 256) sts.
Work 31 rows even as est, then rep *inc row* one more time—160 (176, 192, 212, 228, 244, 260) sts.

Work even as est until body meas 10¼ (10, 9½, 10¼, 9¾, 9½, 10¾)" from underarm, ending after a RS row.

Begin pocket opening with garter stitch trim

Next row: (WS) Work as est to band m, sl m, k4 (5, 7, 9, 9, 9, 10) sl 22 (24, 24, 24, 26, 26, 26) sts to st holder or waste yarn, pm for pocket, using the backward loop cast on, CO 22 (24, 24, 24, 26, 26, 26) sts, pm, knit to m, sl m, knit across back sts, sl m, k5 (6, 8, 11, 13, 17, 20) sts, sl 22 (24, 24, 24, 26, 26, 26) sts to st holder or waste yarn, pm, using the backward loop cast on, CO 22 (24, 24, 24, 26, 26, 26) sts, pm, work to end as est.

Next row *est pocket garter st:* (RS) *Work as est to pocket m, sl m, work to next pocket m in garter st, sl m; rep from * one more time, work to end as est.

Cont as est working body in Rev St st, and bands and pocket trim in garter st until pocket trim measures approx 2" from opening, ending after a WS row.

Remove pocket markers and last increase row for side shaping

Next row *inc row:* (RS) Work as est to pocket m, remove m, purl to next pocket m, remove m, *work to 3 sts before side m, p1-f/b, p2, sl m, p2, p1-f/b, rep from * one time, work to pocket m, remove m, purl to next pocket m, remove m, work to end as est (4 sts inc'd)—164 (180, 196, 216, 232, 248, 264) body sts.
Cont as est working body in Rev St st and bands in garter st until 12 (12, 12, 14, 14, 14, 16) rows are worked even after the 6th buttonhole (body meas approx 15¼ (15, 14½, 15¼, 14¾, 14½, 15¾)" from underarm), ending after a RS row.

Begin garter st edge

Next row: (WS) Sl 1 wyib, knit to end.
Rep last row (working the last buttonhole as est) until garter st meas approx 3" (body meas approx 18¼ (18, 17½, 18¼, 17¾, 17½, 18¾)" from underarm), ending after a RS row.

Next row: (WS) BO all sts knitwise.

Sleeves

Transfer 46 (46, 50, 54, 58, 60, 64) held sts from one sleeve to larger circ, do not join; work back and forth in rows.
Note: Change to larger, straight needles when comfortable, if desired.

Next row: (WS) Using backward loop cast on, CO 4 (5, 5, 6, 6, 7, 7) sts, work in Rev St st to end, CO another 4 (5, 5, 6, 6, 7, 7) sts—54 (56, 60, 66, 70, 74, 78) sts.

Cont in Rev St st until sleeve meas approx 1" from underarm, ending after a WS row.

Begin sleeve shaping

Note: Two sleeve length options are available here. Work for ¾ length or full length sleeves as desired.

For ¾ length sleeves:

Next row *dec row:* (RS) P2, p2tog, purl to last 4 sts, ssp, p2 (2 sts dec'd)—52 (54, 58, 64, 68, 72, 76) sts.
Work 19 rows even in Rev St st.
Rep last 20 rows one more time, then work *dec row* again—48 (50, 54, 60, 64, 68, 72) sts rem.

Cont even in Rev St st until sleeve meas 8" from underarm, ending after a RS row.

For Full length sleeves:

Next row *dec row:* (RS) P2, p2tog, purl to last 4 sts, ssp, p2 (2 sts dec'd)—52 (54, 58, 64, 68, 72, 76) sts.
Work 11 rows even in Rev St st.

Next row: (RS) Rep *dec row* (2 sts dec'd)—50 (52, 56, 62, 66, 70, 74) sts.
Work 13 rows even in Rev St st.
Rep last 14 rows three more times, then work *dec row* again—42 (44, 48, 54, 58, 62, 66) sts rem.

Cont even in Rev St st until sleeve measures 14½" from underarm, ending after a RS row.

For both sleeve lengths:

Change to smaller needle.

Begin garter stitch cuff

Next row: (WS) Knit.
Cont in garter st until cuff measures 4", ending after a RS row.

Next row: (WS) Loosely BO sts knitwise.

Work second sleeve the same as the first.

Pocket linings
Transfer 22 (24, 24, 24, 26, 26, 26) held sts from one pocket to larger straight needle ready to work a RS row.

Next row: (RS) Using the backward loop cast on, CO 1 st, purl to end, CO 1 more st—24 (26, 26, 26, 28, 28, 28) sts.

Cont in Rev St st for 5", ending after a RS row.

Next row: (WS) BO all sts knitwise.

Work second pocket lining the same as the first.

Finishing
Sew pocket linings to inside of sweater. Sew sleeves and underarms. Sew buttons opposite buttonholes. Steam- or wet-block to measurements.

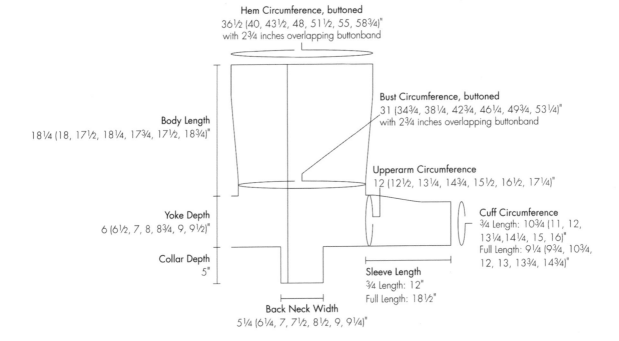

Hem Circumference, buttoned
36½ (40, 43½, 48, 51½, 55, 58¾)"
with 2¾ inches overlapping buttonband

Body Length
18¼ (18, 17½, 18¼, 17¾, 17½, 18¾)"

Bust Circumference, buttoned
31 (34¾, 38¼, 42¾, 46¼, 49¾, 53¼)"
with 2¾ inches overlapping buttonband

Upperarm Circumference
12 (12½, 13¼, 14¾, 15½, 16½, 17¼)"

Yoke Depth
6 (6½, 7, 8, 8¾, 9, 9½)"

Cuff Circumference
¾ Length: 10¾ (11, 12, 13¼,14¼, 15, 16)"
Full Length: 9¼ (9¾, 10¾, 12, 13, 13¾, 14¾)"

Collar Depth
5"

Sleeve Length
¾ Length: 12"
Full Length: 18½"

Back Neck Width
5¼ (6¼, 7, 7½, 8½, 9, 9¼)"

laurel cowl

Finished Measurements
8½" wide and 56" circumference

Yarn
Terra by The Fibre Co.
40% baby alpaca, 40% merino wool, 20% silk;
98 yds / 50g
• 4 skeins in Yarrow
OR 395 yds in worsted weight yarn

Needles
• One pair straight needles in size US 8 [5 mm]
• One spare in same size for three-needle bind off

Or size to obtain gauge

Notions
• Waste yarn
• Tapestry needle

Gauge
18 sts and 36 rows = 4" in garter st, blocked.

Cowl
With waste yarn and using the provisional cast on,
CO 38 sts.
Change to main yarn.

Begin garter stitch
First row: (WS) Knit.
Knit 2 more rows, ending after a WS row.

Begin short row shaping
**Short Row 1: (RS) Knit to last 4 sts, wrap and turn.
Short Row 2: Knit to end.
Short Row 3: Knit to last 7 sts, wrap and turn.
Short Row 4: Knit to end.
Short Row 5: Knit to last 10 sts, wrap and turn.

Short Row 6: Knit to end.
Short Row 7: Knit to last 13 sts, wrap and turn.
Short Row 8: Knit to end.
Short Row 9: Knit to last 16 sts, wrap and turn.
Short Row 10: Knit to end.
Short Row 11: Knit to last 19 sts, wrap and turn.
Short Row 12: Knit to end.
Short Row 13: Knit to last 22 sts, wrap and turn.
Short Row 14: Knit to end.
Short Row 15: Knit to last 25 sts, wrap and turn.
Short Row 16: Knit to end.
Short Row 17: Knit to last 28 sts, wrap and turn.
Short Row 18: Knit to end.
Short Row 19: Knit to last 31 sts, wrap and turn.
Short Row 20: Knit to end.
Short Row 21: Knit to last 34 sts, wrap and turn.
Short Row 22: Knit to end.

Next row: (RS) Knit to end without picking up wraps.
Knit 2 rows, ending after a RS row.
Next row: (WS) Rep Short Row 1.
Rep Short Rows 2–22.
Next row: (WS) Knit to end without picking up
wraps.
Knit 2 rows, ending after a WS row.

Rep from ** until cowl meas 56" from beg, ending
after a WS row.

Unzip provisional cast on and transfer to open
needle. With RS facing and using the three-needle
bind off, join ends to form a loop.

Finishing
Weave in ends. Wet-block to measurements.

liv

Finished Measurements
30¼ (33¾, 37¼, 41, 44½, 48, 51½, 54¼, 57¾)" at bust
Shown in size 33¾" with ¾" positive ease

Yarn
Canopy Worsted by The Fibre Company
50% baby alpaca, 30% merino wool, 20% viscose from bamboo; 200yd /100g
• 5 (5, 6, 6, 7, 7, 8, 8, 9) skeins in Obsidian
OR 950 (1005, 1200, 1280, 1380, 1505, 1610, 1735) yds worsted weight yarn

Needles
• One 16" and 32" circular needle (circ) or longer in size US 6 and 7 [4 and 4.5 mm]
• One set of double-pointed needles (dpns) in size US 6 and 7 [4 and 4.5 mm]

Or size to obtain gauge

Notions
• Stitch markers
• Stitch holder or waste yarn
• CC waste yarn in similar weight for Sunday short rows
• Tapestry needle

Gauge
18 sts and 26 rows = 4" in St st with larger needle, blocked.

Notes
Cardi yoke and body are worked back and forth in rows from the top down. Circular needle is used to accommodate large number of sts. Band is picked up and knitted after body is complete.

Cardi
Yoke
With shorter, larger circ, CO 44 (44, 44, 46, 46, 46, 48, 48, 50) sts. Do not join.

Begin stockinette stitch
First row *place markers:* (WS) P2 for left front, pm, p8 (6, 4, 4, 4, 4, 4, 4, 4) for sleeve, pm, p24 (28, 32, 34, 34, 34, 36, 36, 38) for back neck, pm, p8 (6, 4, 4, 4, 4, 4, 4, 4) for sleeve, pm, p2 for right front.

Begin raglan shaping
Notes: Increases for raglan shaping and center front shaping are worked at the same time, at a different rate. Read the instructions completely and carefully before beginning raglan shaping. Change to longer, larger circ when necessary.
Row 1 *raglan inc row:* (RS) *Knit to one st before m, k1-r/b, sl m, k1, k1-r/b; rep from * three more times (8 sts inc'd)—52 (52, 52, 54, 54, 54, 56, 56, 58) sts.

Row 2: Purl.

Row 3 *center front inc row:* (RS) K2, m1-R, work raglan shaping as est, knit to last 2 sts, m1-L, k2 (2 sts inc'd for center front and 8 sts inc'd for raglan shaping)—62 (62, 62, 64, 64, 64, 66, 66, 68) sts.

Rep *center front inc row* every 4th row 21 (21, 22, 23, 23, 23, 24, 25, 26) more times, **and at the same time,** rep *raglan inc row* every other row 14 (17, 18, 20, 21, 26, 28, 30, 32) more times, then every 4th row 2 (1, 2, 2, 2, 0, 0, 0, 0)—60 (68, 76, 82, 84, 90, 96, 100, 106) sts for back, 44 (46, 48, 52, 54, 60, 64, 68, 72) sts for each sleeve.

Sizes 30¼, 33¾, 37¼ and 41" only:
Skip to All Sizes.

Sizes - (-, -, -, 44½, 48, 51½, 54¼, 57¾)" only:
Next row *body only inc row:* (RS) *Work to 1 sts before m, k1-r/b, sl m, work to m, sl m, k1, k1-r/b; rep from * one more time, work to end—(4 sts inc'd).

Rep *body only inc row* every other row - (-, -, -, 2, 3, 3, 1, 0) more time(s), then every row - (-, -, -, 0, 0, 0, 3, 5) times ; working WS rows as *purl to 1 st before m, p1-f/b, sl m, p1, p1-f/b; rep from * three more times, purl to end— - (-, -, -, 90, 98, 104, 110, 118) sts for back.

All Sizes
Work 1 WS row even.

Begin underarm cast-on
Next row: (RS) Work as est to m, remove m, transfer next 44 (46, 48, 52, 54, 60, 64, 68, 72) sleeve sts to stitch holder or waste yarn, remove m, using backward loop cast on, CO 8 (8, 8, 10, 10, 10, 12, 12, 12) underarm sts, knit back sts to m, remove m, transfer next 44 (46, 48, 52, 54, 60, 64, 68, 72) sleeve sts to stitch holder or waste yarn, remove m, using the backward loop cast on, CO 8 (8, 8, 10, 10, 10, 12, 12, 12) underarm sts, work as est to end—68 (76, 84, 92, 100, 108, 116, 122, 130) sts for back.

Body
Cont in St st and working *center front increases* as est until body meas approx 7½ (7¼, 7, 6¾, 5¾, 5, 5, 5, 5)" from underarm cast on, ending after a center front increase row—160 (172, 186, 202, 218, 234, 250, 264, 280) sts; 46 (48, 51, 55, 59, 63, 67, 71, 75) sts for each front, 68 (76, 84, 92, 100, 108, 116, 122, 130) sts for back.

Work 1 WS row even.

Begin front shaping short rows
Short Row 1: (RS) Knit to 4 sts before end of row, turn work, place one strip of CC yarn across working yarn as for a Sunday Short Row.

Short Row 2: Purl to 4 sts before end of row, turn work, place one strip of CC yarn across working yarn as for a Sunday Short Row.

Short Row 3: Knit to 4 sts before previous turning point, turn work, place one strip of CC yarn across working yarn.

Short Row 4: Purl to 4 sts before previous turning point, turn work, place one strip of CC yarn across working yarn.

Rep Short Rows 3–4 eight more times.

After final turning point, knit to end of row and resolve short rows as for a RS row.

Purl 1 row and resolve short rows as for a WS row.

Begin garter stitch trim and continue center front increases
Next row: (RS) K1, m1-R, knit to last st, m1-L, k1 (2 sts inc'd)—162 (174, 188, 204, 220, 236, 252, 266, 282) sts.

Knit 3 rows.

Rep last 4 rows six more times, garter st trim meas approx 3¼"—174 (186, 200, 216, 232, 248, 264, 278, 294) sts.

Knit 1 RS row even.

Next row: (WS) Loosely BO sts knitwise.

Sleeves
Transfer 44 (46, 48, 52, 54, 60, 64, 68, 72) held sts to larger dpns, dividing sts as evenly as possible. Attach yarn and pick up and knit 4 (4, 4, 5, 5, 5, 6, 6, 6) sts in first 4 (4, 4, 5, 5, 5, 6, 6, 6) underarm sts, pm for BOR, pick up and knit 4 (4, 4, 5, 5, 5, 6, 6, 6) sts in rem underarm sts. Join to begin working in the rnd—52 (54, 56, 62, 64, 70, 76, 80, 84) sts.

Begin underarm shaping
First rnd: Knit.

Cont in St st until sleeve meas approx 2" from underarm.

Begin sleeve shaping
Next rnd *dec rnd:* (RS) K2, k2tog, knit to last 4 sts, ssk, k2 (2 sts dec'd)—50 (52, 54, 60, 62, 68, 74, 78, 82) sts.

Rep *dec rnd* every 14th rnd 4 (4, 4, 0, 0, 0, 0, 0, 0) more times, every 12th rnd 1 (1, 1, 0, 0, 0, 0, 0, 0) time(s), every 10th rnd 0 (0, 0, 2, 2, 0, 0, 0, 0) times, every 8th rnd 0 (0, 0, 6, 6, 1, 0, 0, 0) time(s), every 6th rnd 0 (0, 0, 0, 0, 10, 8, 4, 2) times, then every 4th rnd 0 (0, 0, 0, 0, 0, 5, 11, 14) times—40 (42, 44, 44, 46, 46, 48, 48, 50) sts rem.
Cont even in St st until sleeve meas approx 13" from underarm.

Change to smaller dpns.

Begin garter stitch
Next rnd: Purl.
Cont even in garter st until cuff meas 5", sleeve meas approx 18" [46 cm] from underarm, ending after a purl rnd.

Next rnd: Loosely BO all sts knitwise.

Finishing
Block to measurements.

Band
With smaller, longer circ, RS facing, at the lower edge of right front, pick up and knit 2 sts for every 3 rows.
First row: (WS) Knit.
Cont in garter st until band meas 3¼", ending after a RS row.

Next row: BO all sts knitwise.

Weave in loose ends. Steam-block band if desired.

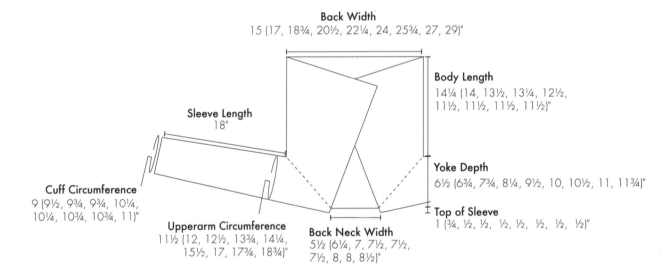

Back Width
15 (17, 18¾, 20½, 22¼, 24, 25¾, 27, 29)"

Body Length
14¼ (14, 13½, 13¼, 12½, 11½, 11½, 11½, 11½)"

Sleeve Length
18"

Yoke Depth
6½ (6¾, 7¾, 8¼, 9½, 10, 10½, 11, 11¾)"

Cuff Circumference
9 (9½, 9¾, 9¾, 10¼, 10¼, 10¾, 10¾, 11)"

Upperarm Circumference
11½ (12, 12½, 13¾, 14¼, 15½, 17, 17¾, 18¾)"

Back Neck Width
5½ (6¼, 7, 7½, 7½, 7½, 8, 8, 8½)"

Top of Sleeve
1 (¾, ½, ½, ½, ½, ½, ½, ½)"

louise top down

Finished Measurements
32¾ (36, 39, 42¼, 45½, 48¾, 52, 55, 58¼)"
bust circumference, buttoned.
Shown in size 36" with 1" of positive ease

Yarn
Osprey by Quince & Co.
100% American wool; 170yd / 100g
- **Color A:** 4 (5, 5, 5, 6, 6, 7, 7, 7) skeins in
  Kumlien's Gull
- **Color B:** 1 (1, 2, 2, 2, 2, 2, 2, 2) skeins
  in Kittywake
- **Color C:** 1 skein in Sabine

OR
- **Color A:** 590 (655, 710, 770, 850, 930,
995, 1060, 1150) yds aran weight yarn
- **Color B:** 145 (150, 160, 170, 180, 190, 200,
210, 220) yds aran weight yarn
- **Color C:** 70 (75, 80, 80, 85, 90, 95, 95, 100)
yds aran weight yarn

Needles
- One 24" circular needle (circ) in sizes US 9 and
  US 10 [5.5 and 6 mm]
- One set of 5 double-pointed needles (dpns) in size
  US 9 and US 10 [5.5 and 6 mm]

Or size to obtain gauge

Notions
- Stitch markers (4)
- Stitch holders or waste yarn
- Tapestry needle
- Six 1" buttons

Gauge
15 sts and 22 rows/rnds = 4" in St st with larger
needle, blocked.

1x1 rib, worked in rows (multiple of 2 sts + 3)
Row 1: (WS) P1, *p1, k1; rep from * to last 2
sts, p2.
Row 2: (RS) K2, *p1, k1; rep from * to last st, k1.
Rep Rows 1 and 2 for pattern.

1x1 rib, worked in the rnd (multiple of 2 sts)
Rnd 1: *K1, p1; rep from * to end.
Rep Rnd 1 for pattern.

Notes
Cardigan is worked from the top down. Circular
needle is used to accommodate large number of sts.
Do not join.

Cardigan

Yoke

With Color A, using larger circ and the long tail cast on, CO 47 sts. Do not join.

Begin stockinette stitch

First row *place markers:* (WS) P2 sts for left front, pm, p8 (8, 8, 6, 6, 6, 4, 4, 4) sts for sleeve, pm, p27 (27, 27, 31, 31, 31, 35, 35, 35) sts for back, pm, p8 (8, 8, 6, 6, 6, 4, 4, 4) for sleeve, pm, p2 for right front.

Begin raglan shaping

Next row *raglan inc row:* (RS) *Knit to one st before m, k1-r/b, sl m, k1, k1-r/b; rep from * three more times, knit to end (8 sts inc'd)—55 sts.
Next row: Purl.

Begin raglan and neck shaping

Next row *neck and raglan inc row:* (RS) K2, m1-L, *knit to one st before m, k1-r/b, sl m, k1, k1-r/b; rep from * three more times, knit to last 2 sts, m1-R, k2 (10 sts inc'd)—65 sts.
Next row: Purl.
Rep last 2 rows three more times—95 sts; 11 sts each front, 18 (18, 18, 16, 16, 16, 14, 14, 14) sts each sleeve and 37 (37, 37, 41, 41, 41, 45, 45, 45) sts for back.

Cast on for neck

Next row: (RS) *Knit to 1 st before m, k1-r/b, sl m, k1, k1-r/b; rep from * 3 more times, knit to end, then using the backward loop cast on, CO 2 (2, 2, 3, 3, 3, 4, 4, 4) sts [10 (10, 10, 11, 11, 11, 12, 12, 12) sts inc'd]—105 (105, 105, 106, 106, 106, 107, 107, 107) sts.
Next row: Purl to end, CO 2 (2, 2, 3, 3, 3, 4, 4, 4) sts—107 (107, 107, 109, 109, 109, 111, 111, 111) sts; 14 (14, 14, 15, 15, 15, 16, 16, 16) sts each front, 20 (20, 20, 18, 18, 18, 16, 16, 16) sts each sleeve and 39 (39, 39, 43, 43, 43, 47, 47, 47) sts for back.

Next row: (RS) *Knit to 1 st before m, k1-r/b, sl m, k1, k1-r/b; rep from * three more times, knit to end, then using the backward loop cast on, CO 3 (3, 3, 4, 4, 4, 5, 5, 5) sts [11 (11, 11, 12, 12, 12, 13, 13, 13) sts inc'd]—118 (118, 118, 121, 121, 121, 124, 124, 124) sts.

Next row: Purl to end, CO 3 (3, 3, 4, 4, 4, 5, 5, 5) sts—121 (121, 121, 125, 125, 125, 129, 129, 129) sts; 18 (18, 18, 20, 20, 20, 22, 22, 22) sts each front, 22 (22, 22, 20, 20, 20, 18, 18, 18) sts each sleeve and 41 (41, 41, 45, 45, 45, 49, 49, 49) sts for back.

Cont raglan shaping

Next row *raglan inc row:* (RS) *Knit to 1 st before m, k1-r/b, sl m, k1, k1-r/b; rep from * three more times, knit to end (8 sts inc'd)—129 (129, 129, 133, 133, 133, 137, 137, 137) sts.
Next row: Purl.
Rep the last 2 rows 1 (7, 10, 9, 12, 15, 16, 17, 17) more times—137 (185, 209, 205, 229, 253, 265, 273, 273) sts; 20 (26, 29, 30, 33, 36, 39, 40, 40) sts each front, 26 (38, 44, 40, 46, 52, 52, 54, 54) sts each sleeve and 45 (57, 63, 65, 71, 77, 83, 85, 85) sts for back.

[Rep *raglan inc row*, then work 3 rows even in St st] 5 (2, 0, 2, 1, 0, 1, 0, 0) time(s)—177 (201, 209, 221, 237, 253, 273, 273, 273) sts; 25 (28, 29, 32, 34, 36, 40, 40, 40) sts each front, 36 (42, 44, 44, 48, 52, 54, 54, 54) sts each sleeve and 55 (61, 63, 69, 73, 77, 85, 85, 85) sts for back.

For Sizes - (-, -, -, -, -, -, 55, 58¼)" only:

Next row *raglan inc row:* (RS) *Knit to 1 st before m, k1-r/b, sl m, k1, k1-r/b; rep from * three more times, knit to end (8 sts inc'd)—281 sts.
Next row *raglan inc row:* (WS) *Purl to 1 st before m, p1-f/b, sl m, p1, p1-f/b; rep from * three more times, purl to end (8 sts inc'd)—289 sts.
Rep the last 2 rows - (-, -, -, -, -, -, 0, 1) more time(s)— - (-, -, -, -, -, -, 289, 305) sts; - (-, -, -, -, -, -, 42, 44) sts each front, - (-, -, -, -, -, -, 58, 62) sts each sleeve and - (-, -, -, -, -, -, 89, 93) sts for back.

For Sizes - (-, 39, 42¼, 45½, 48¾, 52, 55, 58¼)" only:

Next row *body only inc row:* (RS) *Knit to 1 st before m, k1-r/b, sl m, knit to next m, sl m, k1, k1-r/b; rep from * one more time, knit to end (4 sts inc'd)— - (-, 213, 225, 241, 257, 277, 293, 309) sts.
Next row: (WS) Purl.
Rep the last 2 rows - (-, 1, 0, 1, 2, 0, 1, 2) more time(s)— - (-, 217, 225, 245, 265, 277, 297, 317) sts; - (-, 31, 33, 36, 39, 41, 44, 47) sts each front, - (-, 44, 44, 48, 52, 54, 58, 62) sts each sleeve and - (-, 67, 71, 77, 83, 87, 93, 99) sts for back.

All Sizes:
Yoke meas approx 7 (7, 7½, 8¼, 9, 9¾, 10, 10¼, 11)" from back neck to underarm.

Separate body and sleeve stitches, CO for underarm
Next row: (RS) Knit to m, remove m, place next 36 (42, 44, 44, 48, 52, 54, 58, 62) sleeve sts onto waste yarn or stitch holder, remove m, using the backward loop cast on, CO 3 (3, 3, 4, 4, 4, 5, 5, 5) sts, pm for side, CO 3 (3, 3, 4, 4, 4, 5, 5, 5) more sts, knit across 55 (61, 67, 71, 77, 83, 87, 93, 99) back sts, remove m, place next 36 (42, 44, 44, 48, 52, 54, 58, 62) sleeve sts onto waste yarn or stitch holder, remove m, using the backward loop cast on, CO 3 (3, 3, 4, 4, 4, 5, 5, 5) sts, pm for side, CO 3 (3, 3, 4, 4, 4, 5, 5, 5) more sts, knit to end—117 (129, 141, 153, 165, 177, 189, 201, 213) sts, 61 (67, 73, 79, 85, 91, 97, 103, 109) sts for back, 28 (31, 34, 37, 40, 43, 46, 49, 52) sts for each front.

Body
Cont in St st with Color A until body meas 2¼ (2, 2, 1¾, 1½, 1½, 1¼, 1, 1)" from the underarm, ending after a WS row.

Begin waist shaping, decreases
Next row dec row: (RS) *Knit to 3 sts before m, ssk, k1, sl m, k1, k2tog; rep from * one time, knit to end (4 sts dec'd)— 113 (125, 137, 149, 161, 173, 185, 197, 209) sts rem.

Work 9 rows even, then rep dec row—109 (121, 133, 145, 157, 169, 181, 193, 205) sts rem.

Cont even in St st until body meas 6 (5¾, 5¾, 5½, 5¼, 5¼, 5, 4¾, 4¾)" from underarm, ending after a WS row.

Begin side shaping, increases
Next row inc row: (RS) *Knit to 1 st before m, m1-R, k1, sl m, k1, m1-L; rep from * one time, knit to end (4 sts inc'd)—113 (125, 137, 149, 161, 173, 185, 197, 209) sts.

Work 11 rows even, then rep inc row—117 (129, 141, 153, 165, 177, 189, 201, 213) sts.

Cont even in St st until body meas 10½" from underarm, ending after a WS row.

Lower band
Change to Color B.
Next row: (RS) Knit.

Work in 1x1 rib until lower band meas 3½", body meas 14" from underarm, ending after a WS row.

Next row: BO all sts in pattern.

Sleeves
Transfer 36 (42, 44, 44, 48, 52, 54, 58, 62) held sts from 1 sleeve onto larger dpns, and divide as evenly as possible onto 4 dpns. Attach yarn (Color A) and pick up and knit 3 (3, 3, 4, 4, 4, 5, 5, 5) sts in first underarm CO sts, pm for BOR, pick up and knit 3 (3, 3, 4, 4, 4, 5, 5, 5) sts in rem 3 (3, 3, 4, 4, 4, 5, 5, 5) underarm CO sts, join to begin working in the rnd—42 (48, 50, 52, 56, 60, 64, 68, 72) sts.

First rnd: Knit.
Cont in St st in the rnd until sleeve meas 2½ (1¾, 1¾, 1¾, 1¾, 1¾, 1¾, 1¾, 1¾)" from underarm.

Begin sleeve shaping
Next rnd dec rnd: K2, ssk, knit to last 4 sts, k2tog, k2 (2 sts dec'd)—40 (46, 48, 50, 54, 58, 62, 66, 70) sts.

[Knit 13 (11, 11, 11, 9, 9, 9, 7, 5) rnds, then rep dec rnd] 4 (5, 5, 5, 6, 2, 2, 3, 10) times—32 (36, 38, 40, 42, 54, 58, 60, 50) sts rem.

[Knit 0 (0, 0, 0, 0, 7, 7, 5, 0) rnds, then rep dec rnd] 0 (0, 0, 0, 0, 5, 5, 6, 0) times—32 (36, 38, 40, 42, 44, 48, 48, 50) sts rem.

Cont in St st in the rnd until sleeve meas 13½" from underarm.

Cuff
Change to smaller dpns and Color C.
Next rnd: Knit.

Work in 1x1 rib in the rnd until cuff meas 5", sleeve meas 18½" from underarm.

Next rnd: BO all sts in pattern.

Work second sleeve the same as the first.

Finishing
Weave in ends. Steam- or wet-block to measurements.

Neck band
With RS facing, smaller circ and Color B, beg at right front, pick up and knit 15 (15, 15, 17, 17, 17, 19, 19, 19) right front sts, 8 (8, 8, 6, 6, 6, 4, 4, 4) sleeve sts, 27 (27, 27, 31, 31, 31, 35, 35, 35) back neck sts, 8 (8, 8, 6, 6, 6, 4, 4, 4) sleeve sts, and 15 (15, 15, 17, 17, 17, 19, 19, 19) left front sts—73 (73, 73, 77, 77, 77, 81, 81, 81) sts. Do not join.

Work in 1x1 rib until neck band meas 1½" from pick-up row, ending after a WS row.
Next row: BO all sts in pattern.

Buttonhole band
With RS facing, smaller circ and Color B, beg at lower edge of right front, pick up and knit 67 (67, 69, 71, 74, 77, 78, 79, 82) sts (approx 2 sts for every 3 rows) evenly along right front edge. Do not join.

Begin garter stitch
First row: (WS) Knit.
Knit 4 more rows, ending after a WS row.

Buttonhole row: (RS) K6 (6, 4, 5, 4, 6, 6, 7, 6), *[yo] two times, k2tog, k9 (9, 10, 10, 11, 11, 11, 11, 12); rep from * 4 more times, [yo] two times, k2tog, knit to end.

Next row: (WS) Knit to end, dropping second yo for each buttonhole.
Knit 3 more rows, ending after a RS row.
Next row: BO all sts knitwise.

Button band
With RS facing, smaller circ and Color B, beg at neck edge of left front, pick up and knit 67 (67, 69, 71, 74, 77, 78, 79, 82) sts (about 2 sts for every 3 rows) evenly along left front edge. Do not join.

First row: (WS) Knit.
Knit 9 more rows, ending after a RS row.
Next row: BO all sts knitwise.

Block again if desired. Sew buttons opposite buttonholes.

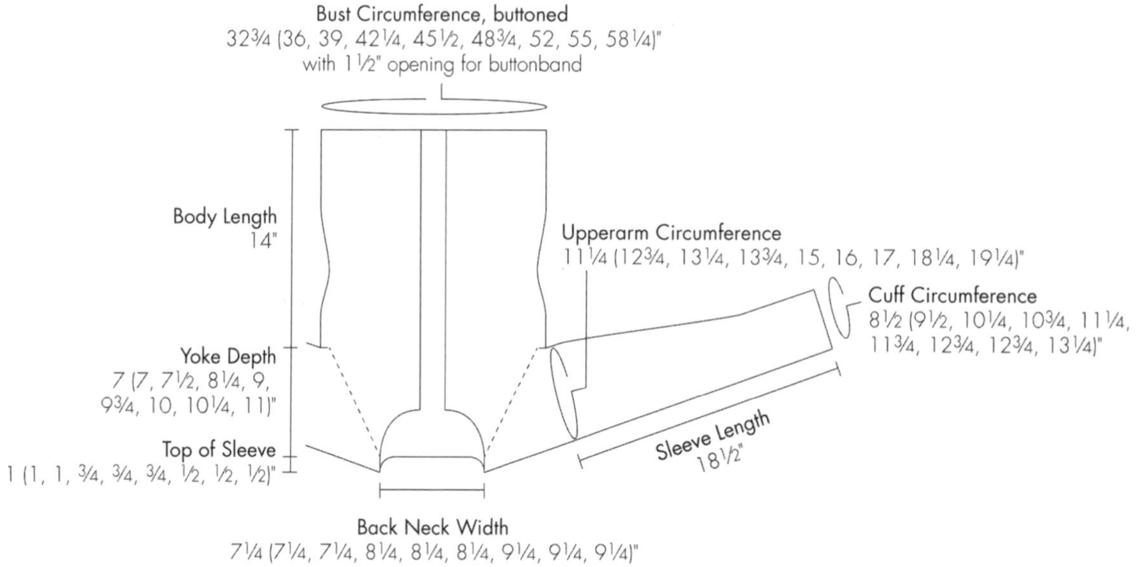

Bust Circumference, buttoned
32¾ (36, 39, 42¼, 45½, 48¾, 52, 55, 58¼)"
with 1½" opening for buttonband

Body Length
14"

Upperarm Circumference
11¼ (12¾, 13¼, 13¾, 15, 16, 17, 18¼, 19¼)"

Cuff Circumference
8½ (9½, 10¼, 10¾, 11¼, 11¾, 12¾, 12¾, 13¼)"

Yoke Depth
7 (7, 7½, 8¼, 9, 9¾, 10, 10¼, 11)"

Top of Sleeve
1 (1, 1, ¾, ¾, ¾, ½, ½, ½)"

Sleeve Length
18½"

Back Neck Width
7¼ (7¼, 7¼, 8¼, 8¼, 8¼, 9¼, 9¼, 9¼)"

madeline

Finished Measurements
33¾ (36¼, 39¾, 43, 46¼, 49¾, 53, 56¼, 59¾)" bust circumference, buttoned with 1" overlapping buttonband
Shown in size 36¼" with 3¼" positive ease (as shown on model on pages 36–37)

Yarn
Chickadee by Quince & Co.
100% American wool; 181yd / 50g
- **Color A:** 8 (8, 9, 9, 10, 11, 12, 13, 14) skeins in Kumlien's Gull
- **Color B:** 1 skein in Iceland

OR
- **Color A:** 1320 (1420, 1510, 1610, 1730, 1870, 2030, 2140, 2310) yds sport weight yarn
- **Color B:** 140 (140, 150, 150, 150, 155, 155, 160, 160) yds sport weight yarn

Needles
- One 40" circular needle (circ) in sizes US 5 and US 6 [3.75 and 4 mm]
- One pair in sizes US 5 [3.75 mm]

Or size to obtain gauge

Notions
- Stitch markers (4)
- Stitch holders or waste yarn
- Tapestry needle
- Eight ½" buttons

Gauge
24 sts and 34 rows = 4" in St st with smaller needle, blocked.

Stripe pattern
Row 1: (RS) Knit with Color B.
Row 2: Purl with Color B.
Rows 3–4: Rep Rows 1–2.
Row 5: Knit with Color A.
Row 6: Purl with Color A.
Rows 7–8: Rep Rows 5–6.
Rep Rows 1–8 for stripe pattern.

Notes
Circular needle is used to accommodate large number of stitches. Hoodie is worked from the bottom up in one piece to underarm with inset pockets and raglan yoke shaping. Sleeves are knit flat and joined to the body at the beginning of the yoke.

Hoodie
Pocket linings (make 2)
With Color B, pair of straight needles, and using the long tail cast on, CO 28 sts.

Begin stripe pattern
Work Rows 1–8 of Stripe Pattern four times.

With Color B, BO 1 st at beg of next 2 rows—26 sts rem. Break yarn leaving a 30" tail to sew lining to body. Transfer sts to st holder or waste yarn.

Make second lining the same as the first.

Body
With Color A, larger circ, and using the long-tail cast on, CO 196 (212, 232, 252, 272, 292, 312, 332, 352) sts. Do not join.

Begin 2x2 rib
First row: (WS) P1, *p2, k2; rep from * to last 3 sts, p3.
Next row: (RS) K1, *k2, p2; rep from * to last 3 sts, k3.
Cont in rib as est until pc meas 1" from cast on edge, ending after a WS row.

Change to smaller circ.

Begin stockinette stitch
Next row: (RS) Knit.
Next row: (WS) Purl.
Cont in St st until pc meas 5" from cast on edge, ending after a RS row.

Begin 2x2 rib for pocket trim and make pocket openings
Next row *place markers for pockets:* (WS) P10, pm, p26, pm, knit to last 36 sts, pm, p26, p10.
Next row: (RS) *Knit to pocket m, sl m, [k2, p2] 6 times, k2, sl m; rep from * one time, knit to end.
Next row: (WS) *Purl to pocket m, sl m, [p2, k2] 6 times, p2, sl m; rep from * one time, purl to end.
Rep last 2 rows until pocket rib meas ½", ending after a RS row.

Next row: (WS) *Purl to pocket m, remove m, BO next 26 sts in pattern, remove m; rep from * one time, purl to end.

Next row *attach pocket linings:* (RS) *Knit to pocket opening, return 26 pocket lining sts to LH needle with RS facing, then knit across; rep from * one time, knit to end.

Cont with Color A and St st until pc meas 13½ (13½, 13¼, 13, 12½, 12½, 12½, 12, 12)" from cast on edge, ending after a WS row.

Next row *place markers for sides:* (RS) K48 (52, 57, 62, 67, 72, 77, 82, 87), pm, k100 (108, 118, 128, 138, 148, 158, 168, 178), pm, k48 (52, 57, 62, 67, 72, 77, 82, 87) to end.

Separate fronts and back
Next row: (WS) *Purl to 5 (5, 6, 6, 7, 7, 8, 8, 9) sts before m, BO 10 (10, 12, 12, 14, 14, 16, 16, 18) sts removing m; rep from * one time, purl to end—90 (98, 106, 116, 124, 134, 142, 152, 160) sts rem for back, 43 (47, 51, 56, 60, 65, 69, 74, 78) sts rem for each front.

Keep sts on circ and set aside. Do not break yarn.

Sleeves (make 2)
With Color A, pair of straight needles, and using the long tail cast on, CO 54 (58, 58, 58, 62, 62, 66, 66, 70) sts.

Begin 2x2 rib
First row: (RS) K3, *p2, k2; rep from * to last 3 sts, p2, k1.
Next row: (WS) P1, *k2, p2; rep from * to last 5 sts, k2, p3.
Cont in 2x2 rib as est until sleeve meas 3½" from cast on edge, ending after a WS row.

Begin stockinette stitch
Next row: (RS) Knit.
Next row: (WS) Purl.
Cont in St st until sleeve meas 4½" from cast on edge, ending after a WS row.

Begin sleeve shaping
Next row *inc row:* K2, m1-R, knit to last 2 sts, m1-L, k2 (2 sts inc'd)—56 (60, 60, 60, 64, 64, 68, 68, 72) sts.

[Knit 9 (9, 7, 7, 5, 5, 3, 3, 3) rows, then rep *inc row*] 3 (3, 4, 9, 5, 13, 3, 9, 15) times—62 (66, 68, 78, 74, 90, 74, 86, 102) sts.

[Knit 11 (11, 9, 9, 7, 7, 5, 5, 5) rows, then rep *inc row*] 6 (6, 7, 3, 9, 3, 15, 11, 7) times—74 (78, 82, 84, 92, 96, 104, 108, 116) sts. Work even in St st until sleeve meas 18½" from cast on edge, ending after a WS row.

Begin underarm bindoffs
BO 5 (5, 6, 6, 7, 7, 8, 8, 9) sts at beg of next 2 rows—64 (68, 70, 72, 78, 82, 88, 92, 98) sts rem. Transfer sts to st holder or waste yarn and break yarn.

Work second sleeve the same as the first.

Yoke
Join sleeves to body
Cont working in St st with circ and body sts, joining sleeve sts as follows:
Next row: (RS) K43 (47, 51, 56, 60, 65, 69, 74, 78) front sts, pm, transfer 64 (68, 70, 72, 78, 82, 88, 92, 98) held sleeve sts onto empty needle and knit across, pm, k90 (98, 106, 116, 124, 134, 142, 152, 160) back sts, pm, transfer 64 (68, 70, 72, 78, 82, 88, 92, 98) held sleeve sts onto empty needle and knit across, pm, k43 (47, 51, 56, 60, 65, 69, 74, 78) front sts to end—304 (328, 348, 372, 400, 428, 456, 484, 512) sts.

Work 1 row even.

Begin yoke shaping
Next row *raglan dec row:* (RS) *Knit to 3 sts before m, ssk, k1, sl m, k1, k2tog; rep from * three more times, knit to end (8 sts dec'd)—296 (320, 340, 364, 392, 420, 448, 476, 504) sts.

Size 33¾ (-, -, -, -, -, -, -, -)" only:
[Work 3 rows in St st, then rep *raglan dec row*] one more time—288 sts rem; 41 sts each front, 60 sts each sleeve and 86 sts for back.

All Sizes:
[Purl 1 row, then rep *raglan dec row*] 24 (28, 30, 32, 35, 37, 40, 42, 45) times—96 (96, 100, 108, 112, 124, 128, 140, 144) sts rem; 17 (18, 20, 23, 24, 27, 28, 31, 32) sts each front, 12 (10, 8, 6, 6, 6, 6, 6, 6) sts each sleeve and 38 (40, 44, 50, 52, 58, 60, 66, 68) sts for back.

Sizes - (-, -, 43, 46¼, 49¾, 53, 56¼, 59¾)" only:
Purl 1 WS row.
Next row *front and back only dec row:* (RS) Knit to 3 sts before m, ssk, k1, sl m, knit to next m, sl m, k2tog; rep from * one time, knit to end (4 sts dec'd)— - (-, -, 104, 108, 120, 124, 136, 140) sts rem sts rem. Rep the last 2 rows - (-, -, 1, 2, 4, 5, 7, 8) more time(s)— - - (-, -, 100, 100, 104, 104, 108, 108) sts rem; - (-, -, 21 (21, 22, 22, 23, 23) sts each front, - (-, -, 6, 6, 6, 6, 6, 6) sts each sleeve and - (-, -, 46, 46, 48, 48, 50, 50) sts for back.

All Sizes:
Next row *place marker:* (WS) K48 (48, 50, 50, 50, 52, 52, 54, 54) removing raglan markers, pm for center of hood, k48 (48, 50, 50, 50, 52, 52, 54, 54) to end, removing raglan markers.

Hood
Begin stripe pattern
Work Rows 1–8 of Stripe Pattern 8 times, then work Rows 1–4 one more time; hood meas 8".

Cont to work stripe pattern as est and at the same time, begin hood shaping:
Next row *dec row:* (RS) Knit to 3 sts before m, ssk, k1, sl m, k1, k2tog, knit to end (2 sts dec'd)—94 (94, 98, 98, 98, 102, 102, 106, 106) sts rem.

[Work 5 rows even, then rep *dec row*] 2 times—90 (90, 94, 94, 94, 98, 98, 102, 102) sts rem.

[Work 3 rows even, then rep *dec row*] 5 times—80 (80, 84, 84, 84, 88, 88, 92, 92) sts rem.

[Work 1 row even, then rep *dec row*] 4 times—72 (72, 76, 76, 76, 80, 80, 84, 84) sts rem.

Next row: (RS) Rep *dec row* —70 (70, 74, 74, 74, 78, 78, 82, 82) sts rem.
Next row *dec row:* (WS) Purl to 3 sts before m, p2tog, p1, sl m, p1, ssp, purl to end—68 (68, 72, 72, 72, 76, 76, 80, 80) sts rem.
Rep the last 2 rows one time—64 (64, 68, 68, 68, 72, 72, 76, 76) sts rem.

Work 1 WS row, ending after Row 2 of stripe pattern; hood meas 13½" from beg of hood.

Close hood
Next row: (RS) Place sts onto 2 needles, dividing evenly, and removing m. Join hood using the three-needle bind off.

Finishing
Weave in ends. Wet-block to measurements. Sew sleeves and seam underarms. Whip stitch sides of pocket lining to body.

Front band
With smaller circ, Color A and RS facing, beg at lower right front edge, pick up and knit 96 (98, 100, 102, 104, 108, 112, 116, 120) sts evenly to beg of hood, pick up and knit 66 sts along right edge of hood to seam, then 66 sts along left edge of hood to body, then pick up and knit another 96 (98, 100, 102, 104, 108, 112, 116, 120) sts evenly along left front edge—324 (328, 332, 336, 340, 348, 356, 364, 372) sts. Do not join; work back and forth in rows.

Begin 2x2 rib
Next row: (WS) P3, *k2, p2; rep from * to last st, p1.

Next row: (RS) K1, *k2, p2; rep from * to last 3 sts, k3.
Work 1 more row in rib as est.

Begin buttonhole row
With RS facing, place removable marker on right front 2" below beg of hood at purl set of rib. Then place 7 more markers evenly spaced on purl sets of rib for buttonhole placement. Hoodie is shown with 8 buttons, but feel free to adjust this as you desire.

Next row: (RS) K3, *p2tog, [yo] 2 times, k2, p2, k2, p2, k2; rep from * 6 more times, p2tog, [yo] 2 times, work in rib as est to end.
Next row: (WS) *Work in rib as est to first buttonhole, knit into yarn over, dropping extra wrap; rep from * 7 more times, work in rib as est to end.

Cont in rib until band meas 1" from pick up row, ending after a WS row.

Next row: BO all sts in pattern.

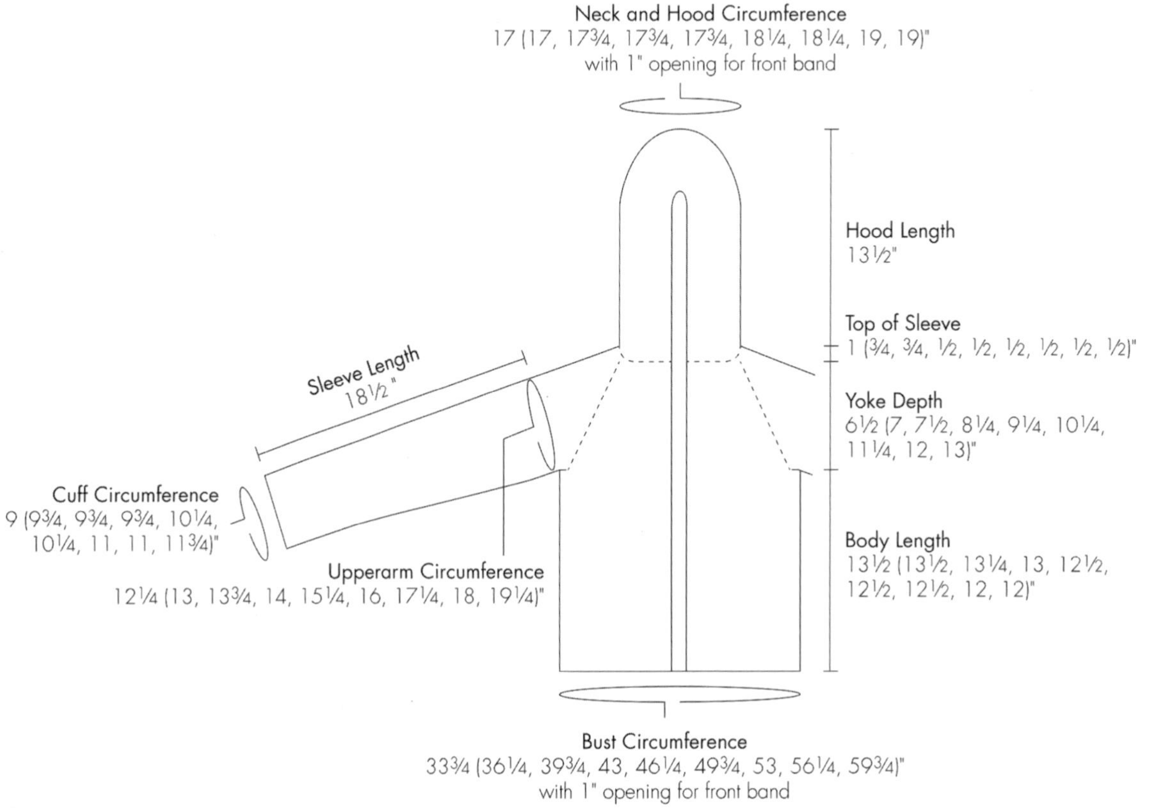

Neck and Hood Circumference
17 (17, 17¾, 17¾, 17¾, 18¼, 18¼, 19, 19)"
with 1" opening for front band

Hood Length
13½"

Top of Sleeve
1 (¾, ¾, ½, ½, ½, ½, ½, ½)"

Yoke Depth
6½ (7, 7½, 8¼, 9¼, 10¼, 11¼, 12, 13)"

Sleeve Length
18½"

Cuff Circumference
9 (9¾, 9¾, 9¾, 10¼, 10¼, 11, 11, 11¾)"

Upperarm Circumference
12¼ (13, 13¾, 14, 15¼, 16, 17¼, 18, 19¼)"

Body Length
13½ (13½, 13¼, 13, 12½, 12½, 12½, 12, 12)"

Bust Circumference
33¾ (36¼, 39¾, 43, 46¼, 49¾, 53, 56¼, 59¾)"
with 1" opening for front band

lucinda

Finished Measurements
37¼ (40¼, 44, 47¾, 51¼, 54¼, 58, 61¾, 64¾, 68½)" bust circumference
Shown in size 44" with shorter sleeves and 10" positive ease (on model above) and on pages 38–39 with 9" positive ease

Yarn
Acadia by The Fibre Co.
60% merino wool, 20% baby alpaca, 20% silk; 145yd / 50g, shown in Oyster

For shorter sleeves:
- 8 (9, 9, 11, 11, 12, 13, 14, 15, 16) skeins OR 1070 (1175, 1305, 1450, 1590, 1725, 1870, 2020, 2135, 2270) yds in dk weight yarn

For longer sleeves:
- 9 (10, 11, 12, 13, 14, 15, 16, 16, 17) skeins OR 1225 (1340, 1465, 1625, 1755, 1900, 2045, 2185, 2315, 2450) yds in dk weight yarn

Needles
- One 16" circular needle (circ) in size US 5 [3.75 mm]
- One 24" circ in sizes US 5 and 6 [3.75 and 4 mm]
- One set of double-pointed needles dpns in size US 4 and 5 [3.5 and 3.75 mm]

Or size to obtain gauge

Notions
- Stitch markers (3)
- Stitch holders or waste yarn
- Tapestry needle
- CC waste yarn in similar weight for Sunday short rows

Gauge
21½ sts and 36 rnds/rows = 4" in Rev St st with middle needle, blocked.

Notes
Lucinda is worked from the bottom up in one piece, then turned right side out at the armhole and worked back and forth in rows. Shoulders are joined using the three-needle bind off. Sleeve stitches are pick up around the armhole and worked in the rnd to the cuff. Pullover is worked inside-out since I find many knitters prefer to knit rather than purl. There are two sleeve length options; sample shown is the shorter version.

Reverse stockinette stitch, flat (Rev St st)
Purl on the RS and knit on the WS.

V-neck Pullover

Body

Begin at hem

Note: Pullover is worked inside-out to the armhole. With longer, larger circ, CO 208 (228, 248, 268, 288, 308, 328, 348, 368, 388) sts. Pm for BOR and join to work in the rnd being careful not to twist sts.

Begin 2x2 rib

First rnd: *K2, p2; rep from * to end.
Rep last rnd until rib meas ½" from cast on edge.

Change to smaller, longer circ.

Begin stockinette stitch in the rnd

Next rnd *dec rnd:* *K20 (4, 2, 12, 20, 8, 2, 12, 2, 12), [k2tog, k18 (16, 18, 18, 18, 16, 18, 18, 16, 16)] 4 (6, 6, 6, 6, 8, 8, 8, 10, 10)] times, k4 (2, 2, 2, 4, 2, 2, 2, 2, 2); rep from * one more time [8 (12, 12, 12, 12, 16, 16, 16, 20, 20) sts dec'd]—200 (216, 236, 256, 276, 292, 312, 332, 348, 368) sts rem.
Next rnd: Knit.
Cont in St st until body meas 16" from cast on edge.

Begin armhole shaping

Next rnd *and place marker for side:* K100 (108, 118, 128, 138, 146, 156, 166, 174, 184), pm for side, knit to end.
Turn work right side out, so the purl side is facing you. Pullover is now worked in Rev St st.

Next row *armhole inc row:* (RS) P1, m1-P, purl to one st before side m, m1-P, p1 (2 sts inc'd)—102 (110, 120, 130, 140, 148, 158, 168, 176, 186) sts for back.

Back

Begin working back and forth in rows

Turn work so the knit side is facing you.
Next row: (WS) P1, knit to last st, p1.
Next row: (RS) K1, purl to last st, k1.
Cont in Rev St st as est until pc meas 2 (2½, 3, 3½, 4, 4½, 5, 5½, 5¾, 6)" from beg of armhole divide.

Begin v-neck shaping

Read through instructions for back carefully. Shoulder shaping begins before neck shaping ends, and both are worked at the same time.

Note: To work right back separately, but at the same time as the left back, a second ball of yarn will be joined at center front.

Next row: (WS) P1, k50 (54, 59, 64, 69, 73, 78, 83, 87, 92), pm (indicating center back), k50 (54, 59, 64, 69, 73, 78, 83, 87, 92), p1.
Next row *center dec row:* (RS) K1, purl to 4 sts before center m, p2tog, p2, remove m, join new ball of yarn to work other side, p2, ssp, purl to last st, k1 (2 sts dec'd)—50 (54, 59, 64, 69, 73, 78, 83, 87, 92) sts each side.
Next row *center dec row:* (WS) P1, knit to 4 sts before neck edge, k2tog, k2, on other side, k2, ssk, knit to last st, p1 (2 sts dec'd)—49 (53, 58, 63, 68, 72, 77, 82, 86, 91) sts each side.
Rep last two rows one more time— 47 (51, 56, 61, 66, 70, 75, 80, 84, 89) sts each side.
Next row *center dec row:* (RS) K1, purl to 4 sts before center m, p2tog, p2, on other side, p2, ssp, purl to last st, k1 (2 sts dec'd)—46 (50, 55, 60, 65, 69, 74, 79, 83, 88) sts each side.
Rep last row every other row 13 (15, 15, 16, 17, 18, 18, 19, 19, 20) more times—33 (35, 40, 44, 48, 51, 56, 60, 64, 68) sts rem on each side;
and at the same time:

Cont in Rev St st until pc meas 5½ (6, 6½, 7, 7½, 8, 8½, 9, 9¼, 9½)" from armhole inc row, ending after a WS row.

Begin shoulder shaping

Short Row 1: (RS) Work as est to neck edge, on other side, work as est to last 4 (4, 5, 3, 6, 3, 7, 4, 7, 5) sts, turn work, place one strip of CC yarn across working yarn as for a Sunday Short Row.
Short Row 2: (WS) Knit to last 4 (4, 5, 3, 6, 3, 7, 4, 7, 5), turn work, place one strip of CC yarn across working yarn as for a Sunday Short Row.
Short Row 3: Work as est to 4 (4, 5, 6, 6, 7, 7, 8, 8, 9) sts before previous turning point, turn work, place one strip of CC yarn across working yarn.
Short Row 4: Knit to 4 (4, 5, 6, 6, 7, 7, 8, 8, 9) sts before previous turning point, turn work, place one strip of CC yarn across working yarn.
Rep Short Rows 3–4 five more times.

After final turning point, purl to end of row and resolve short rows as you come to them for a WS row.

Next row: (WS) Knit and resolve short rows as you come to them for a RS row.

Note: Short rows are resolved in this way since you are working in Rev St st.

Slip sts to waste yarn or stitch holder.

Front

Join yarn ready to work a RS row.

Next row *armhole inc row:* (RS) P1, m1p, purl to one st before side m, m1p, p1 (2 sts inc'd)—51 (55, 60, 65, 70, 74, 79, 84, 88, 93) sts for front.

Begin working back and forth in rows

Turn work so the knit side is facing you.

Next row: (WS) P1, knit to last st, p1.

Next row: (RS) K1, purl to last st, k1.

Work even for 0 (0, 0, 2, 4, 6, 8, 10, 12, 14) rows.

Begin v-neck shaping

Read through instructions for front carefully. Shoulder shaping begins before neck shaping ends, and both are worked at the same time.

Note: To work right front separately, but at the same time as the left front, a second ball of yarn will be joined at center front.

Next row: (WS) P1, k50 (54, 59, 64, 69, 73, 78, 83, 87, 92), pm (indicating center front), k50 (54, 59, 64, 69, 73, 78, 83, 87, 92), p1.

Next row *neck dec row:* (RS) K1, purl to 4 sts before center m, p2tog, p2, remove m, join new ball of yarn to work other side, p2, ssp, purl to last st, k1 (2 sts dec'd)—50 (54, 59, 64, 69, 73, 78, 83, 87, 92) sts each side.

Next row: (WS) P1, knit to center, on other side, knit to last st, p1.

Rep *neck dec row* every RS row 14 (17, 14, 16, 18, 20, 19, 21, 21, 22) more times, every 4th row 2 (1, 4, 3, 2, 1, 2, 1, 1, 1) times, then every 6th row one time—33 (35, 40, 44, 48, 51, 56, 60, 64, 68) sts rem on each side; **and at the same time:**

Cont in Rev St st until pc measures 5½ (6, 6½, 7, 7½, 8, 8½, 9, 9¼, 9½)" from armhole inc row, ending after a WS row.

Begin shoulder shaping

Short Row 1: (RS) Work as est to neck edge, on other side, work as est to last 4 (4, 5, 3, 6, 3, 7, 4, 7, 5) sts, turn work, place one strip of CC yarn across working yarn as for a Sunday Short Row.

Short Row 2: (WS) Knit to last 4 (4, 5, 3, 6, 3, 7, 4, 7, 5), turn work, place one strip of CC yarn across working yarn as for a Sunday Short Row.

Short Row 3: Work as est to 4 (4, 5, 6, 6, 7, 7, 8, 8, 9) sts before previous turning point, turn work, place one strip of CC yarn across working yarn.

Short Row 4: Knit to 4 (4, 5, 6, 6, 7, 7, 8, 8, 9) sts before previous turning point, turn work, place one strip of CC yarn across working yarn.

Rep Short Rows 3–4 five more times.

After final turning point, purl to end of row and resolve short rows as you come to them for a WS row.

Next row: (WS) Knit and resolve short rows as you come to them for a RS row.

Note: Short rows are resolved in this way since you are working in Rev St st.

Slip sts to waste yarn or holder.

Finishing

Weave in ends. Block to measurements.

Join shoulders

Transfer 33 (35, 40, 44, 48, 51, 56, 60, 64, 68) shoulder sts of left front back to needles. With RS of left front and left back facing, use yarn tail and work the three-needle bind off, BO all sts. Rep for right shoulder.

Sleeves

With larger dpns, RS facing, and beg at center st of underarm, pick up and knit 58 (62, 66, 74, 78, 86, 90, 94, 98, 102) sts around armhole for sleeves. Place marker (pm) for beg of rnd (BOR) and join to work in the rnd.

Turn Pullover inside-out.

Begin stockinette st, in the rnd
First rnd: Knit.
Cont in St st in the rnd until sleeve meas 1" from underarm.

For shorter sleeves:
Begin sleeve shaping
Next rnd *dec rnd:* K2, k2tog, knit to last 4 sts, ssk, k2 (2 sts dec'd)— 56 (60, 64, 72, 76, 84, 88, 92, 96, 100) sts.
Rep *dec rnd* every 4th rnd one time, then every 6th rnd 4 times, then every 8th rnd one time— 44 (48, 52, 60, 64, 72, 76, 80, 84, 88) sts rem.
Cont in St st in the rnd until sleeve meas 6½" from underarm.

For longer sleeves:
Begin sleeve shaping
Next rnd *dec rnd:* K2, k2tog, knit to last 4 sts, ssk, k2 (2 sts dec'd)—54 (60, 64, 70, 76, 82, 86, 92, 94, 98) sts.
Rep *dec rnd* every 18th rnd 1 (2, 0, 0, 0, 0, 0, 0, 0, 0) more time(s), every 12th rnd 5 (3, 6, 0, 0, 0, 0, 0, 0, 0), every 10th rnd 0 (1, 2, 8, 0, 0, 0, 0, 0, 0) time(s), every 8th rnd 0 (0, 0, 0, 2, 12, 6, 0, 0, 0) times, every 6th rnd 0 (0, 0, 0, 0, 8, 16, 15, 15, 11) times then every 4th rnd 0 (0, 0, 0, 0, 0, 0, 3, 3, 9) times —44 (48, 48, 52, 52, 56, 56, 56, 60, 60) sts rem.

Cont in St st until sleeve meas 13½" from underarm.

Begin 2x2 rib cuff
Next rnd: *K2, p2; rep from * to end.
Rep last rnd until cuff meas 3".

Change to smaller dpns.

Cont in 2x2 as est until cuff meas 4½"; shorter sleeve meas 11" from underarm and longer sleeve meas 18" from underarm.

Next rnd: BO all sts in pattern.

Rep for second sleeve.

Neck trim
Turn work right side out, so purl side is facing you. With RS facing, at center back neck edge, and smaller, shortest circ, pick up and knit 1 stitch for every bound off neck st, then 2 sts for every 3 rows down left front and around right front, then 1 stitch for every bound off neck st. Place marker for BOR and join to work in the rnd.

Next rnd: Knit.
Next rnd: BO all sts purlwise.

Weave in ends. Block pc again to measurements.

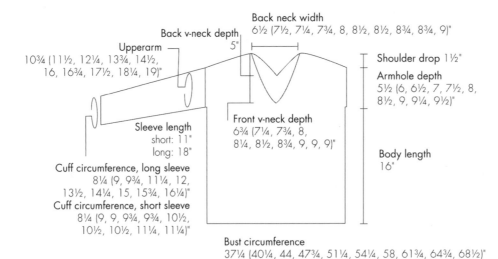

Back neck width
6½ (7½, 7¼, 7¾, 8, 8½, 8½, 8¾, 8¾, 9)"

Back v-neck depth
5"

Upperarm
10¾ (11½, 12¼, 13¾, 14½, 16, 16¾, 17½, 18¼, 19)"

Shoulder drop 1½"

Armhole depth
5½ (6, 6½, 7, 7½, 8, 8½, 9, 9¼, 9½)"

Sleeve length
short: 11"
long: 18"

Front v-neck depth
6¾ (7¼, 7¾, 8, 8¼, 8½, 8¾, 9, 9, 9)"

Body length
16"

Cuff circumference, long sleeve
8¼ (9, 9¾, 11¼, 12, 13½, 14¼, 15, 15¾, 16¼)"
Cuff circumference, short sleeve
8¼ (9, 9, 9¾, 9¾, 10½, 10½, 10½, 11¼, 11¼)"

Bust circumference
37¼ (40¼, 44, 47¾, 51¼, 54¼, 58, 61¾, 64¾, 68½)"

lori shawl

Finished Measurements
52¾" wide and 26½" deep

Yarn
Road to China Light by The Fibre Co.
65% baby alpaca, 15% silk, 10% camel, 10% cashmere; 159yd / 50g
• 5 skeins in Grey Pearl
OR 795 yds sport weight yarn

Needles
• One 32" circular needle in size US 5 [3.75 mm]
Or size to obtain gauge

Notions
• Tapestry needle

Gauge
22 sts and 44 rows = 4" in garter stitch, blocked.

Notes
Shawl is worked from the long edge to the point. Decreases are made on one side to shape the shawl.

Try to work the edge stitches on the decrease side very loosely. If you work them too tightly the shawl will curl. If you have problems working them loosely, work the decrease as (k3tog, yo, k1) instead and drop the yo on the next row.

Shawl
Using the long tail cast on, CO 290 sts. Do not join.

Begin garter stitch
First row: (WS) Knit.
Knit 2 more rows.

Begin shawl shaping
Next row *dec row:* (RS) Sl 1 wyib as if to knit, knit to last 4 sts, k3tog, k1 (2 sts dec'd)—288 sts.
Next row: Sl1, knit to end.
Rep *dec row* every other row 143 more times (286 sts dec'd)—2 sts rem.

Next row: (WS) BO knitwise.

Finishing
Weave in ends. Wet-block to measurements.

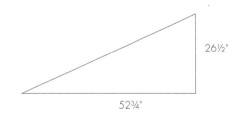

charlotte light cardigan

Finished Measurements
32¾ (35¾, 38½, 41½, 44¼, 48, 51, 54½, 57½)", bust circumference, buttoned
Shown in size 35¾" with ¾" positive ease and A-line shaping

Yarn
Road to China Light by The Fibre Co.
65% baby alpaca, 15% silk, 10% camel, 10% cashmere; 159yd / 50g
• 8 (8, 9, 10, 10, 11, 12, 12, 13) skeins in Hematite
OR 1165 (1265, 1365, 1460, 1555, 1675, 1760, 1880, 1985) yds sport weight yarn
For no A-line shaping, cardigan uses approx 25 fewer yds

Needles
• One 32" circular needle (circ) in size US 5 [3.75 mm]
• One set of double-pointed needles (dpns) in size US 5 [3.75 mm]
Or size to obtain gauge

Notions
• Stitch markers (4)
• Stitch holders or waste yarn
• Tapestry needle
• Four ½" buttons

Gauge
22 sts and 44 rows = 4" in garter stitch, blocked.

Notes
Cardigan is worked from the top down. Circular needle is used to accommodate large number of stitches. Pattern is written with 2 body options: without shaping or with A-line shaping. When working in garter stitch, slip first st of every row as if to knit, while holding yarn in the back.

Cardigan
Yoke
Using the long tail cast on, CO 104 sts. Do not join.

Begin 2x2 rib band
First row: (WS) P1, *p2, k2; rep to last 3 sts, p3.
Next row: (RS) K3, *p2, k2; rep from * to last 5 sts, p2, k3.
Cont in rib as est until band meas approx 1" from cast on edge, ending after a WS row.

Next row *buttonhole row:* (RS) Work rib as est to last 5 sts, yo, p2tog, k3.
Cont in rib as est until band meas approx 2" from cast on edge, ending after a RS row.

Begin yoke shaping and garter stitch

Next row *place markers:* (WS) Sl 1 knitwise wyib, k23 (24, 24, 24, 24, 24, 24, 24, 24) for front, pm, k10 (8, 8, 8, 8, 8, 8, 8, 8) for sleeve, pm, k36 (38, 38, 38, 38, 38, 38, 38, 38) for back, pm, k10 (8, 8, 8, 8, 8, 8, 8, 8) for sleeve, pm, k24 (25, 25, 25, 25, 25, 25, 25, 25) for front.

Next row *inc row:* (RS) Sl 1, *knit to 2 sts before m, k1-f/b, k1, sl m, k1, k1-f/b; rep from * 3 more times, knit to end (8 sts inc'd)—112 sts.

Next row: Sl 1, knit to end.

Rep the last 2 rows 3 more times—136 sts.

Next row *inc row and work buttonhole row 1:* (RS) Sl 1, *knit to 2 sts before m, k1-f/b, k1, sl m, k1, k1-f/b; rep from * 3 more times, knit to last 6 sts, k2tog, (yo) twice, k2tog, k2 (8 sts inc'd)—144 sts.

Next row *buttonhole row 2:* Sl 1, k2, (knit into first yo wrap, knit through the back of second yo wrap), knit to end.

Next row: (RS) Rep *inc row*.

Rep *inc row* every other row 7 (8, 14, 16, 19, 21, 28, 32, 34) more times, then every 4th row 10 (11, 9, 8, 7, 6, 2, 0, 0) times; **and at the same time,** rep *buttonhole rows 1 and 2* two more times approx 2" (same distance as between first two buttonholes) below last buttonhole worked (4 buttonholes total)— 288 (304, 336, 344, 360, 368, 392, 408, 424) sts total; 47 (50, 54, 55, 57, 58, 61, 63, 65) sts each front; 56 (58, 66, 68, 72, 74, 80, 84, 88) sts each sleeve; 82 (88, 96, 98, 102, 104, 110, 114, 118) sts for back.

For Sizes 32¾ (35¾, 38½, -, -, -, -, -, -)" only:

Skip to All Sizes below.

For Sizes - (-, -, -, 41½, 44¼, 48, 51, 54½, 57½)" only:

Next row *body only inc row:* *Work to 2 st before raglan m, k1-f/b, k1, sl m, work to next raglan m, sl m, k1, k1-f/b; rep from * one more time, work to end (4 sts inc'd)— - (-, -, -, 348, 364, 372, 396, 412, 428) sts.

Rep *body only inc row* every other row - (-, -, -, 2, 4, 7, 8, 10, 7) more times, then every row - (-, -, -, 0, 0, 0, 0, 0, 5) more times (working increase on WS rows as p1-f/b) — - (-, -, -, 356, 380, 400, 428, 452, 476) sts.

All Sizes:

47 (50, 54, 58, 62, 66, 70, 74, 78) sts for each front, 56 (58, 66, 68, 72, 74, 80, 84, 88) sts for each sleeve, 82 (88, 96, 104, 112, 120, 128, 136, 144) sts for back; 288 (304, 336, 356, 380, 400, 428, 452, 476) sts total.

Knit 3 (3, 3, 3, 3, 3, 3, 4) rows even, slipping first st of evey row; yoke meas approx 8½ (9, 9¼, 10, 10½, 11, 11, 11¼, 11¾)" from cast on edge.

Separate body and sleeves

Next row: (RS) Sl 1, knit to m, remove m, place next 56 (58, 66, 68, 72, 74, 80, 84, 88) sleeve sts onto waste yarn or stitch holder, remove m, using the backwards loop cast on, CO 4 (5, 5, 5, 5, 6, 6, 7, 7) sts, pm for side, CO 4 (5, 5, 5, 5, 6, 6, 7, 7) more sts, knit across 82 (88, 96, 104, 112, 120, 128, 136, 144) back sts, remove m, place next 56 (58, 66, 68, 72, 74, 80, 84, 88) sleeve sts onto waste yarn or stitch holder, remove m, using the backwards loop cast on, CO 4 (5, 5, 5, 5, 6, 6, 7, 7) sts, pm for side, CO 4 (5, 5, 5, 5, 6, 6, 7, 7) more sts, knit to end—192 (208, 224, 240, 256, 276, 292, 312, 328,) sts total; 90 (98, 106, 114, 122, 132, 140, 150, 158) back sts; 51 (55, 59, 63, 67, 72, 76, 81, 85) front sts.

Body without shaping

Cont as est, slipping first st of each row and working all other sts in garter st until body meas approx 14" from the underarm cast on, ending after a WS row.

Next row: BO loosely knitwise.

Body with A-line shaping

Cont as est, slipping first st of each row and working all other sts in garter st until body meas approx 2" from the underarm cast on, ending after a WS row.

Next row *inc row:* (RS) Knit to 3 sts before side m, k1-f/b, k2, sl m, k2, k1-f/b; rep from * one more time, knit to end (4 sts inc'd)—196 (212, 228, 244, 260, 280, 296, 316, 332) sts.

Rep *inc row* every 24th row 3 more times—208 (224, 240, 256, 272, 292, 308, 328, 344) sts.

Cont as est, slipping first st of each row and working all other sts in garter st until body meas approx 14¼" from the underarm cast on, ending after a WS row.

Next row: Loosely BO all sts knitwise.

Sleeves
Transfer 56 (58, 66, 68, 72, 74, 80, 84, 88) sleeve sts to dpns, and divide as evenly as possible onto 4 dpns. At center of underarm CO sts, attach yarn and pick up and knit 4 (5, 5, 5, 5, 6, 6, 7, 7) sts in first half of underarm CO sts, knit across sleeve sts, pick up and knit 4 (5, 5, 5, 5, 6, 6, 7, 7) sts in rem underarm CO sts. Pm for BOR and join to work in the rnd—64 (68, 76, 78, 82, 86, 92, 98, 102) sts.

Next rnd: Purl.
Next rnd: Knit.
Cont in garter st in the rnd until sleeve meas approx 1½" from underarm, ending after a purl rnd.

Begin sleeve shaping
Next rnd dec rnd: K2, k2tog, knit to last 4 sts, ssk, k2 (2 sts dec'd)—62 (66, 74, 76, 80, 84, 90, 96, 100) sts.

Rep *dec rnd* every 18th rnd 3 (3, 0, 0, 0, 0, 0, 0, 0) times, every 16th rnd 4 (4, 0, 0, 0, 0, 0, 0, 0) times, every 12th rnd 0 (0, 4, 0, 0, 0, 0, 0, 0) times, every 10th rnd 0 (0, 7, 11, 3, 3, 0, 0, 0) times, every 8th rnd 0 (0, 0, 1, 11, 11, 8, 5, 0) time(s), every 6th rnd 0 (0, 0, 0, 0, 0, 9, 13, 19) times, then every 4th rnd 0 (0, 0, 0, 0, 0, 0, 0, 1) time(s)—48 (52, 52, 52, 52, 56, 56, 60, 60) sts rem.
Cont in garter st in the rnd until sleeve meas approx 12¾" from underarm, ending after a purl rnd.

Begin 2x2 rib band
Next rnd: *K2, p2; rep from * to end.
Cont in rib as est until cuff meas approx 5"; sleeve meas approx 17¾" from underarm.

Next rnd: Loosely BO all sts knitwise.

Finishing
Weave in ends. Steam- or wet-block to measurements. Sew buttons opposite buttonholes.

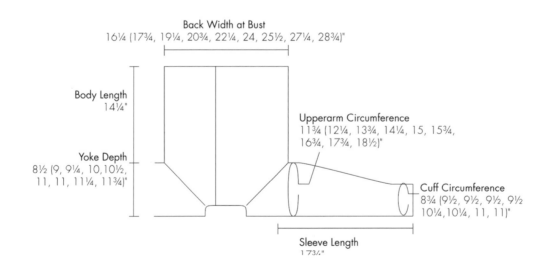

Back Width at Bust
16¼ (17¾, 19¼, 20¾, 22¼, 24, 25½, 27¼, 28¾)"

Body Length
14¼"

Yoke Depth
8½ (9, 9¼, 10, 10½, 11, 11, 11¼, 11¾)"

Upperarm Circumference
11¾ (12¼, 13¾, 14¼, 15, 15¾, 16¾, 17¾, 18½)"

Cuff Circumference
8¾ (9½, 9½, 9½, 9½, 10¼, 10¼, 11, 11)"

Sleeve Length
17¾"

charlotte light accessories

Beret
Finished Measurements
17½" brim circumference
Yarn
Fresco by Classic Elite Yarns
60% wool, 30% baby alpaca, 10% angora;
164yd/50g
- 1 skein in Cinder, Oatmeal, or Parchment

Sample used one entire skein
OR 164 yds fingering weight yarn
Needles
- One set double-pointed needles (dpns) in size
  US 2 and 4 [2.75 and 3.5 mm]

Or size to obtain gauge
Notions
- Stitch marker
- Tapesty needle
Gauge
24 sts and 44 rnds = 4" with larger needles in
garter stitch, blocked.

Beret
With smaller dpns CO 104 sts. Join to work in the
rnd, being careful not to twist sts, place m for BOR.

Begin 2x2 Rib
First rnd: *K2, p2; rep from * to end.
Work as est in rib until pc meas approx 1¼".

Next rnd *inc rnd:* P3, *p2, p1-f/b, p3, p1-f/b; rep
from * to last 3 sts (28 sts incd)—132 sts.

Change to larger needles.

Begin garter stitch pattern
Next rnd: Knit.
Next rnd: Purl.
Cont in garter st until beret meas approx 5¾" from
the beg, ending after a purl rnd.

Shape crown
Rnd 1 *dec rnd:* *K9, ssk; rep from * (12 sts
dec'd)—120 sts.
Rnd 2 and all even rnds: Purl.
Rnd 3 *dec rnd:* *K8, ssk; rep from * (12 sts
dec'd)—108 sts.
Rnd 5 *dec rnd:* *K7, ssk; rep from * (12 sts
dec'd)—96 sts.
Rnd 7 *dec rnd:* *K6, ssk; rep from * (12 sts
dec'd)—84 sts.
Rnd 9 *dec rnd:* *K5, ssk; rep from * (12 sts
dec'd)—72 sts.

Rnd 11 *dec rnd:* *K4, ssk; rep from * (12 sts dec'd)—60 sts.
Rnd 13 *dec rnd:* *K3, ssk; rep from * (12 sts dec'd)—48 sts.
Rnd 15 *dec rnd:* *K2, ssk; rep from * (12 sts dec'd)—36 sts.
Rnd 17 *dec rnd:* *K1, ssk; rep from * (12 sts dec'd)—24 sts.
Rnd 19 *dec rnd:* *Ssk; rep from * (12 sts dec'd)—12 sts.
Rnd 21 *dec rnd:* *Ssk; rep from * (6 sts dec'd)—6 sts rem.
Rnd 22: Purl.

Finishing
Break yarn and thread through remaining sts, pull tight. Weave in ends and block.

Mitts
Finished Measurements
7½" circumference at widest point of hand
Yarn
Pure Blends Fingering by Swans Island
85% organic merino, 15% alpaca; 525yd /100g
• 1 skein in Seasmoke
OR 200 yds fingering weight yarn
Needles
• One set of double-pointed needles (dpns) in size US 3 [3.25 mm]
Or size to obtain gauge
Notions
• Stitch markers (3)
• Waste yarn for holding live stitches
• Tapestry needle
Gauge
26 sts and 52 rnds = 4" in garter stitch, blocked.

Mitts
CO 48 sts. Divide sts evenly onto 4 dpns, place marker and join to work in the rnd, being careful not to twist sts.

Begin 2x2 rib
First rnd: *K2, p2; rep from * to end.
Rep last rnd until mitts meas 7½" from cast on edge.

Begin garter stitch
Next rnd: Purl.
Next rnd: Knit.

Cont in garter st for 5 more rnds, ending after a purl rnd.

Thumb gusset for right mitten
Set up rnd *place markers:* K23, pm, m1-L, k2, m1-R, pm, knit to end (2 sts inc'd)—50 sts.
Work 5 rnds in garter st.
Next rnd *inc rnd:* Knit to first m, sl m, m1-L, knit to 2nd marker, m1-R, sl m, knit to end of rnd (2 sts inc'd)—52 sts.
Cont in garter st and rep *inc rnd* every 6th rnd four more times—60 sts; 14 sts between markers.

Divide for thumb
Next rnd: Purl to 1st m, remove m, purl to 2nd m, remove m. Place the 14 sts that have just been worked onto waste yarn (these were the sts between your markers), then purl to end of rnd—48 sts rem on needles.
Next rnd: Knit to held thumb sts, CO 2 sts using firm backward loop cast on, knit to end—50 sts.
Work 5 rnds even in garter st, ending after a purl rnd.

Begin 2x2 rib
Next rnd: *K2, p2; rep from * to end of rnd.
Rep last rnd until rib meas ½".

Next rnd: BO all sts in rib pattern.

Thumb
Place held thumb sts onto dpns.
Next rnd: Pick up and knit 2 sts from backward loop cast on sts on hand, knit to end—16 sts.
Work 5 rnds even in garter st, ending after a purl rnd.

Begin 2x2 rib
Next rnd: *K2, p2; rep from * to end of rnd.
Rep last rnd until rib meas ½".

Next rnd: BO all sts in rib pattern.

Rep for second mitt.

Finishing
Block mitts to measurements. Weave in ends.

Scarf
Finished Measurements
8¾" wide and 62" long
Yarn
Road to China Light by The Fibre Co.
65% baby alpaca, 15% silk, 10% camel,
10% cashmere; 159yd / 50g
- 3 skeins in Riverstone

Sample used three entire skeins
Needles
- One pair in size US 5 [3.75 mm]

Or size to obtain gauge
Gauge
22 sts and 44 rows = 4" in garter stitch, blocked.

Scarf
Using the long tail cast on, CO 48 sts.

Begin 2x2 rib
First row: (WS) P1, *p2, k2; rep to last 3 sts, p3.
Next row: (RS) K3, *p2, k2; rep from * to last st k1.
Cont in rib as est until rib meas 7" from cast on
edge, ending after a RS row.

Begin garter stitch
Next row: (WS) Sl 1 st knitwise wyib, knit to end.
Cont in garter st as est until scarf meas approx 55"
from cast on edge, ending after a RS row.

Begin 2x2 rib on other end
Next row: (WS) P1, *p2, k2; rep to last 3 sts, p3.
Next row: (RS) K3, *p2, k2; rep from * to last
st, k1.
Cont in rib as est until rib meas 7"; scarf meas 62"
from cast on edge, ending after a RS row.
Next row: BO all sts in pattern.

Finishing
Weave in ends. Wet-block to measurements.

ABBREVIATIONS

approx: approximately
beg: begin(ning)
BO: bind off
BOR: beginning of round
circ: circular
CC: contrasting color
CO: cast on
cont: continue
dec('d): decrease(d)
dpns: double-pointed needles
est: establish(ed)
inc('d): increase(d)
k: knit
k1-f/b: knit into front and back of next st (1 st increased).
k1-r/b: Slightly twist work on LH needle towards you so that WS of work is visible. Insert RH needle from top down into next st on LH needle one row below. Knit this st then knit st on LH needle (1 st increased).
k2tog: knit 2 sts together (1 st decreased).
k3tog: Knit 3 sts together (2 sts decreased, leans to the right).
LH: left hand
m: marker
m1 (make 1): Insert LH needle from front to back under horizontal strand between st just worked and next st, knit lifted strand through the back loop (1 st increased).
m1-L (make 1 left slanting): Insert left needle from front to back under horizontal strand between st just worked and next st, knit lifted strand through the back loop (1 st increased).
m1-P (make 1 purlwise): Insert LH needle under horizontal strand between st just worked and next st, from the back to the front, purl (1 st increased).

m1-R (make 1 right slanting): Insert left needle from back to front under horizontal strand between st just worked and next st, knit lifted strand through the front loop (1 st increased).
meas: measure(s)
p: purl
p1-f/b (purl 1, front and back): Purl into the front loop, then the back loop of next st (1 st increased).
p1-r/b: Insert RH needle from top down into next st on LH needle one row below. Purl this st then purl st on LH needle (1 st increased).
p2tog: Purl 2 sts together (1 st decreased).
pc: piece(s)
pm: place marker
rem: remain
rep: repeat
rnd: round
RH: right hand
RS: right side
sl: slip
ssk (slip, slip, knit): Slip 2 sts one at a time knitwise to the right needle; return sts to left needle in turned position and knit them together through the back loops (1 st decreased).
ssp (slip, slip, purl): Slip 2 sts one at a time knitwise to the right needle; return sts to left needle in turned position and purl them together through the back loops (1 st decreased).
st(s): stitch(es)
St st: stockinette stitch
WS: wrong side
wyib: with yarn in back
wyif: with yarn in front
yo: yarn over

cheryl brunette.com
brunette

One row button hole

Step 1: Work to buttonhole marker. Slip the next stitch purlwise and bring the yarn to the front. *Slip another stitch and pass the previous slipped stitch over (1 st is bound off); rep from *until you have bound off the desired number of stitches (do not use working yarn to bind off).

Step 2: Slip the last stitch on the RH needle back to the LH needle and turn the work around (WS facing you). Bring yarn to the front of work. Insert the RH needle purlwise into the first stitch on the left hand needle. *Wrap yarn around as if to purl and pull up a loop, place this twisted loop onto LH needle (1 stitch has been cast on); rep from *until you have cast on the number of stitches that were bound off plus one additional stitch.

Step 3: Turn the work again (RS facing). Slip the first stitch from the LH needle to the RH needle and pass the extra cast on sts over. Slip the last stitch on the RH needle back to the LH needle and continue to knit as established.

Three-Needle Bind Off

Divide sts evenly over 2 needles; with the RS of garment pcs together (to form ridge on inside of garment), hold the needles parallel. With a third needle knit the first st of front and back needles together, *knit next st from each needle together, (2 sts on RH needle), BO 1 st; rep from * until all sts are BO.

w&t (wrap and turn) short rows in garter stitch

Slip the next st to the RH needle and bring the yarn to the front of work between the needles. Slip st back to the LH needle. Turn, ready to knit next row wyib.

Stockinette stitch flat
Knit on RS, purl on WS.

Stockinette stitch in the rnd
Knit every rnd.

Garter stitch flat
Knit every row.

Garter stitch in the rnd
Rnd 1: Purl.
Rnd 2: Knit.
Rep Rnds 1 and 2 for garter st in the rnd.

Backward loop cast on
*Wrap yarn around left thumb from front to back and secure in palm with other fingers. Insert needle upwards through strand on thumb. Slip loop from thumb onto right needle, pulling yarn to tighten; rep from * for indicated number of sts.

Sunday Short Rows
http://www.sundayknits.com/techniques/shortrows.html

Long tail cast on
http://www.knitty.com/ISSUEsummer05/FEAT-sum05TT.html

Provisional cast on
http://www.knitty.com/ISSUEfall05/FEATfall05TT.html

For...

My girls, Imogen and Sigrid, for inspiring me daily.

Thanks...

The knitters: Sue Macurdy, Nicole Dupuis, Peter Kennedy, Ann Kearsley, Cecily Glowik MacDonald, Allie Matthews, Dawn Catanzaro, Shanna Lovelace, Sierra Roberts, and Larisa Norman.

The tech editors: Kristen TenDyke & Dawn Catanzaro.

The models: Chloe Cekada, Ashley Letizia, and Hannah Dennitz.

The locations: And thank you, coast of Maine, for being such a gorgeous backdrop.

About...

Carrie Bostick Hoge is a knitwear designer and photographer based in Maine. She is the self-published author of the *Madder Anthology* book series. Carrie's designs have also been published in Brooklyn Tweed's *Wool People, Amirisu, Taproot Magazine, Interweave Knits, Knitscene, New England Knits, Fair Isle Style,* and on Quince & Co.'s website.

www.maddermade.com